Violence in Sports

Other titles in the Issues in Focus *series:*

AIDS
Choices for Life
ISBN 0-89490-903-7

ALTERNATIVE MEDICINE
Is It for You?
ISBN 0-89490-955-X

BODY IMAGE
A Reality Check
ISBN 0-89490-960-6

CULTS
ISBN 0-89490-900-2

DRUG TESTING
An Issue for School,
Sports, and Work
ISBN 0-89490-954-1

FAMILY ABUSE
A National Epidemic
ISBN 0-89490-720-4

GUNS, VIOLENCE, AND TEENS
ISBN 0-89490-721-2

THE INTERNET
Surfing the Issues
ISBN 0-89490-956-8

MILITIAS
Armed and Dangerous
ISBN 0-89490-902-9

NEO-NAZIS
A Growing Threat
ISBN 0-89490-901-0

PLAGUE AND PESTILENCE
A History of Infectious
Disease
ISBN 0-89490-957-6

PORNOGRAPHY
Debating the Issues
ISBN 0-89490-907-X

PRISONS
Today's Debate
ISBN 0-89490-906-1

SCHOOL PRAYER
A History of the Debate
ISBN 0-89490-904-5

SCHOOLS UNDER SIEGE
Guns, Gangs, and Hidden
Dangers
ISBN 0-89490-908-8

SEXUAL HARASSMENT
What Teens Should Know
ISBN 0-89490-735-2

TEEN CRIME WAVE
A Growing Problem
ISBN 0-89490-910-X

TEEN SMOKING
Understanding the Risk
ISBN 0-89490-722-0

WOMEN IN COMBAT
The Battle for Equality
ISBN 0-7660-1103-8

Violence in Sports

Victory at What Price?

Jeffrey A. Margolis

Enslow Publishers, Inc.

40 Industrial Road   PO Box 38
Box 398   Aldershot
Berkeley Heights, NJ 07922 Hants GU12 6BP
USA   UK

http://www.enslow.com

Dedication

*This book is dedicated to the athletes representing the
State of Israel who were senselessly murdered during the 1972
Summer Olympic Games in Munich, Germany. We should
never lose sight of the true role of games in our society:
fairness, respect for one's opponent, and graciousness
in winning or losing.*

Library of Congress Cataloging-in-Publication Data

Margolis, Jeffrey A.
    Violence in sports : victory at what price? / Jeffrey A.
    Margolis
        p. cm. — (Issues in focus)
    Includes bibliographical references (p. 115) and index.
    Summary: Discusses the issues related to manifestations of
    violent behavior in sports at all levels of competition and the
    effect of this violence on society in general.
      ISBN 0-89490-961-4
      1. Violence in sports—United States—Juvenile literature.
    2. Sports—Social aspects—United States—Juvenile literature.
    [1.Violence in sports.] I. Title. II. Series: Issues in focus
    (Hillside, N.J.)
    GV706.7 .M37 1998
    796'.0973—ddc21   98-35031
                                          CIP
                                          AC

Printed in the United States of America

10 9 8 7 6 5 4 3 2 1

To Our Readers:
All Internet addresses in this book were active and appropriate when we went to
press. Any comments or suggestions can be sent by e-mail to Comments @enslow.
com or to the address on the back cover.

Illustration Credits: © Allsport USA, pp. 23, 29, 30, 32, 45, 50, 88, 96, 104;
AP/Wide World Photos, p. 6; © Corel Corporation, pp. 18, 35, 55, 107; Dallas
Cowboys, p. 67; Jeffrey A. Margolis, pp. 27, 37, 60; J.G. Heck. *The Complete
Encyclopedia of Illustration.* New York: Park Lane, 1979, pp. 15, 16; National
Archives, pp. 78, 85.

Cover Illustration: Allen Eyestone, *The Palm Beach Post.* On the cover, the
Miami Heat's Alonzo Mourning (Number 33) is restrained by New York
Knickerbockers' coach Jeff Van Gundy (bottom), as he pushes the Knicks'
Charles Oakley (Number 34).

Contents

Challenger Mike Tyson (left) brutally bites the ear of heavyweight champion Evander Holyfield during a June 1997 boxing match in Las Vegas, Nevada.

1

Introduction

Although sports have been around since man's civilization has been recorded, perhaps at no time in history have people's appetites for their games been as ravenous as they are today. Never before have sports occupied so large a place in people's hearts, minds, and pocketbooks. In addition, although violence has always been associated with sports, never before have games promoted such widespread acts of violence, both on and off the field.

Professional sports, particularly football, baseball, basketball, ice hockey, and boxing, can fill a void in peoples' lives.

The games provide excitement in an otherwise routine existence. Many sociologists and psychologists note that we live in an intensely competitive age and that, therefore, sports competition is merely an extension of the general culture.

Most sports necessarily involve aggressive behavior. Football and hockey demand brutal physical contact by their players that is a necessary part of the games. And although it is illegal for us to beat each other senseless on the street, people seem glad to watch others do it legally in sports. They will even pay dearly to see this conflict happen. According to sociologist Stanley Eitzen, sports have even become a substitute for war. He theorizes that when Air Force jets fly in formation over a stadium during a halftime show, it subliminally sends the message: There is a link between sports and combat.[1]

A spokesman for the National Football League once commented,

> Why is professional football so popular? It's a physical contact sport. I think it's what society wants. They want to see contact sports. It's something that goes back to the gladiator days. Why did people go to the Colosseum in Rome to see gladiators fight? Because it is a very physical thing. [Now] instead of fighting with swords, we're fighting with padded bodies.[2]

Bob Clarke, general manager of the Philadelphia Flyers hockey team said, "If they cut down on violence too much, people won't come out to watch. It's a reflection of our society. People want to see violence."[3] It is interesting to note that Clarke was captain of the Flyers when they were known as the notorious "Broad Street Bullies" in the 1970s. The team's fighting and aggressive style of play caused the National Hockey League to change its rules.

Why have sports today become so violent? Basically, the main object of any sporting event is to score more goals, run faster, and break existing records.[4] However, psychiatrist Arnold Beisser sees it another way. He observes, "The good competitor uses his opponent as a temporary enemy. He may even appear angry at him; some good competitors seem to require grudge opponents."[5] Many psychologists believe that the competition to win, at any price, in a business that has grown to billion-dollar proportions, has lessened the ideals of true sportsmanship.

Sports as Big Business

Of all the factors that have affected the role of sports in this country, money has been the most crucial. Sports is big business in America. Today, athletes—sometimes right out of high school—earn millions of dollars a year in salaries as well as in product endorsement fees. The athletes are able to command such large salaries because quality sports talent is a highly saleable commodity. Superstar athletes like Michael Jordan, who are instantly recognizable and widely idolized, draw millions of fans to the stadiums and courts. Because such sports stars sell so many tickets, their salaries seem justified to team owners and managers—the stars are attracting more money for their teams than they are earning in their salaries, and the teams are reaping a huge profit.

There is no doubt that money has affected the attitude of the players. Today's athletes have become like the hired gunfighters of the old west— their loyalty changes according to who is signing their checks. Few players are traded anymore, especially without their consent, because of the policy of free agency. Instead, the players sign short-term contracts for huge sums of money, and at the end of the contract's term, they declare themselves to be free agents, offering their services to the highest bidder. This practice has led to a decline in team spirit and a lack of team cohesion. Thirty years ago, a player would have spent his entire career with one team, and his loyalty to that team and his teammates would be unwavering.

The athletes are not the only ones concerned with making as much money as possible. Team owners have insisted that cities build huge multimillion-dollar stadiums outfitted with luxury box seats to attract the fans and to maximize the income from ticket sales. In addition, expensive computer technology installed at the stadiums broadcasts replays and paid advertisements on giant-screen television monitors. This advertising is paid for by corporate sponsors. Revenue from the television networks that are broadcasting the events across the country is also a major factor in a team's ultimate financial success. Financially speaking, this revenue can be more important than a team's won-lost record.

Several teams are actually public companies—

ordinary people can buy shares of stock in them. The National Basketball Association's (NBA) Boston Celtics, the National Hockey League's (NHL) Florida Panthers, and the National Football League's (NFL) Green Bay Packers are examples. Other teams are owned outright by large corporations. The Walt Disney Company owns the Mighty Ducks and the Anaheim Angels, and the Tribune newspaper company owns baseball's Chicago Cubs. To their large corporate sponsors, the teams represent an investment and need to show a profit, thus raising the stakes in professional sports.

Stressed Out

All this pressure for a team to win brings stress to the players both on and off the field. Sometimes players relieve this stress by fighting during a game or by becoming violent at home. Some athletes have resorted to alcohol and drug abuse. Others have committed serious crimes.

Aggressive behavior both on and off the field has caused some athletes serious injuries and tragic personal setbacks. Football players like Dennis Byrd and Marc Buoniconti have been paralyzed as a result of athletic injuries. Boxers Benny Paret and Duk Koo Kim died after receiving injuries in the ring. Out of the ring, former heavyweight fighter Mike Tyson molested a beauty pageant contestant and spent six years in prison.

Although there have been isolated complaints about the change in the value system of today's athletes and how their behavior is affecting young people, there has been no significant public protest about the current rules in professional sports or about the way athletes behave. Can Bob Clarke, general manager of the Flyers, be right—that fans prefer their sports to be violent? Perhaps, after reading every day in our newspapers about shootings, rapes, and drug-related crimes we have come to expect the same jolt of sensational violence from our sports.

The issue of violence in modern sports raises many interesting questions: Has the degree of violence in modern athletic competition increased because more violence is what the fans want to see? Or have athletes, accustomed to being treated like royalty, gotten out of control? Most important, what, if anything, can we do to restore our time-honored standards of sportsmanship and fair play?

2

A Short History of Violence in Sports

Violence in sports is not new. It can be traced back to the earliest sports in the earliest civilizations. Archaeologists have uncovered drawings on ancient pottery and on the walls of caves depicting athletes competing in sports, some of them extremely combative.

Ancient History

The Olympic Games were born in ancient Greece. They included many sports events and competitions. Boxing was introduced in 688 B.C. and became popular with both the athletes and the spectators of that era.

13

One event, called pankration, was introduced into the Olympics in 648 B.C.[1] It was highlighted by an all-out fight between two combatants. Under the ancient rules devised by the Greeks, boxing, kicking, and strangleholds were tactics allowed in the sport. However, biting and gouging of an opponent were grounds for disqualification.

Chariot racing was also introduced during the Olympic Games at approximately the same time. Crashes were common, and many racers were killed when the teams of horses pulling their chariots accidentally trampled the drivers underfoot.

Violence and death reached a new level, however, with the Roman civilization. The first gladiator events began around 246 B.C. Huge colosseums were built to accommodate the overflowing crowds that loved both the spectacle of the sport and the inevitable bloodshed that accompanied it.

The gladiators were trained warriors and athletes who fought against each other, two at a time, to entertain the people of Rome. The weapons they used included swords and spears, and the combatants usually kept fighting until one of them was killed. However, the life of the loser might be spared if the crowd felt he had fought an outstandingly valiant fight or if a politically well-connected young lady took a liking to his efforts. Although most were either prisoners, slaves, or criminals, some freemen competed for money as well as for fame.

Other events that pitted slaves and prisoners against wild animals in a contest to the death were also very popular with the people. These cruel battles, the Romans rationalized, would harden its citizens to the sight of bloodshed, thereby making them better able to wage war. Finally, around A.D. 404, Emperor Honorius banned gladiator combat.[2]

In the Americas, between 800 and 300 B.C., the local people developed a vicious ball game, the object of which was to drive a solid rubber ball through a stone ring. According to researchers, the captain of the losing team was routinely beheaded. In 1519, when the Spanish explorer Cortez landed in what is now Mexico, he is said to have found more than 135,000 skulls in the Aztec capital.[3]

Events that pitted animals against slaves and prisoners were a popular Roman spectacle.

In England, during the Middle Ages, tournaments and jousts were the most popular sportslike diversions. During these tournaments knights gathered together and fought each other in a type of medieval war game. The losers had to pay the winners with items of value. Because the injuries and incidents of property destruction resulting from the tournaments were so numerous and severe, both the English government and the Church eventually had them banned.

Jousts became popular in the 1200s. At jousting matches, local townspeople flocked to see two opposing knights on horseback charge at each other, each holding a lance. Originally, the sport was meant to be harmless. The knights' lances were supposed to be blunted to prevent serious injury. However, by the end of the century, spike-tipped lances replaced the blunted tips, and knights, despite their suits of

Jousts and other tournaments during the Middle Ages frequently ended in death. Here, a man waits with a coffin (bottom left) ready for the knight who will lose.

armor, were commonly injured and even killed during the matches.[4]

Middle History

By the eighteenth century, fencing duels had become a popular bloodsport attraction. These duels soon gave way to bare-knuckle boxing matches. This primitive version of boxing drew villagers for miles around, not only to witness the fights, but also to place bets on the outcome. Many fighters suffered permanent injuries. Some of the contestants died as a result of these injuries, which commonly went untreated. Nevertheless, the popularity of the sport continued, due in large part to a notion that boxing was an acceptable way for an Englishman to prove his manhood.

Eventually, boxing was imported from England to the colonies in America where it also became popular. Since the sport was illegal, many of the early bouts took place in the back rooms of local taverns. Later, during the Civil War, boxing grew in popularity as a diversion for the soldiers.

During the eighteenth century, the sport of bullfighting became popular with spectators in Spain. The first permanent ring was built for bullfighting at that time. A special breed of bull was developed especially for these events. In a bullfight the matador, or "killer," and his assistants first taunt the bull. Then, they try to weaken him. Finally, the matador, displaying his skills with a cloth and sword, kills the bull. Although the bull is killed in almost all cases, there are still numerous incidents in which the matador is seriously harmed or even gored to death by the bull's horns.

Modern History

Even by the twentieth century, when men were considered "civilized," violence remained a part of their sports. In the early 1900s, baseball legend Ty Cobb of the Detroit Tigers earned a reputation for fighting with players on the opposing teams, as well

Bullfighting remains a popular spectator sport in many Spanish-speaking countries. In Spain and Mexico, most bullfighters are considered national heroes.

as with his own teammates. Decades later, Yankee legend Billy Martin received wide-scale publicity for his aggressive antics both on and off the baseball diamond. Nowadays both men's displays of temper seem tame in comparison with todays tantrums.

During the last thirty years, the behavior and attitudes of some star athletes at both the professional and collegiate levels have changed. The actions of sports figures like heavyweight boxing champion Muhammad Ali seemed outrageous in the 1960s when he boasted, "I am the Greatest." Today Ali's poetic outbursts seem merely distinctive and amusing. Outrageous is a term more aptly applied to NBA star Dennis Rodman, who frequently changes the color of his hair and dresses in women's clothing. The term is also more fitting for college basketball star Len Bias and the NFL's Lyle Alzado who turned to the use of drugs. Both of them are now dead.

Longtime diehard fans who used to be able to gain easy access to their favorite sports idols now note that many athletes have hired bodyguards to keep fans at a distance. Many professional players now also charge money for their autographs, a courtesy they used to extend to fans for free. In addition, some players have taken offensive action against spectators: During the 1981 season, baseball player Cesar Cedeno ran into the stands at Atlanta Fulton County Stadium and grabbed a baseball fan who had been heckling him. Cedeno received a suspension from the league.[5]

The changes in the public's attitude toward their sports heroes have also made their way into films. In

1975, *Rollerball*, a satire about sports violence, depicted a brutal game during which the number of players killed and injured was listed on the scoreboard, along with the score of the game. Another film, *Slap Shot*, concerned a small-town minor-league ice hockey team that rose to the top by using cheap shots and starting brawls with their opponents.

Sports play a huge role in America's culture. The games we watch and the athletes who play them reflect who we are as a society. What is the message our sports are giving us today? As violence has intensified in the United States, so has the level of violence in its sports.

The role of drugs has also intensified in American sports. Athletes take drugs to reduce pain and to improve on-the-field performance. They also take illegal drugs to feel good, even though they know taking drugs is prohibited by college and professional league regulations.

Violence in Pro Sports

Mike Utley played professional football for the Detroit Lions. He had been a college All-American from Washington State University and was drafted by the Lions in 1989. During a game against the Los Angeles Rams on November 17, 1991, Utley, while playing his position at right guard, suffered an injury that fractured two of his vertebrae. The injury left him paralyzed. Although he has undergone surgery and endured countless hours of physical therapy since the accident, Utley is still disabled, working hard to be able to walk again.[1]

Violent Injuries in Football

Violent play has taken an exacting toll on many other athletes, as well. Merril Hoge was a running back for almost eight years. For seven of them, he played football for the Pittsburgh Steelers, and for almost a year he played for the Chicago Bears. During the 1994 season, Hoge received four concussions within a span of five weeks. Years later, he continues to suffer from painful headaches. He also experiences some memory loss, and he is sometimes unable to recognize members of his own family.

Hoge is one of several pro football players suffering from postconcussion syndrome, an injury only recently labeled and recognized by the NFL. This condition is caused by receiving a second concussion when a prior one has not fully healed. Hoge's successive concussions caused him to retire as a football player much earlier than he expected.[2]

During the 1992 season, more than four hundred eighty football players were injured seriously enough to miss at least one game. According to a report in *Sports Illustrated* magazine, on the average, seventeen players on each NFL team are injured each season.[3] Injuries are bound to happen when three-hundred-pound linemen career into two-hundred-fifty-pound running backs on a regular basis.

Basketball Fouls

For the 1978–79 season, in response to increasing on-the-court violence, the National Basketball

Association decided to add a third referee for each game. His job is to help reduce or eliminate the number of flagrant fouls that occur during a game. However, this change did not succeed in ending all on-court violence.

On January 16, 1988, during a basketball game between the Chicago Bulls and the Detroit Pistons, Rick Mahorn of the Pistons fouled Michael Jordan of the Bulls. Teammate Charles Oakley rushed to Jordan's aid, and a brawl broke out. Mahorn received a five-thousand-dollar fine and a one-game suspension from the commissioner of the league. But

Pile-ups involving numerous players, like this one involving the Dallas Cowboys and the Green Bay Packers, can often cause injuries, especially for the players on the bottom.

this story was not unusual. By the halfway point in the season, fourteen players had received fines ranging from seven hundred fifty to five thousand dollars. Five of these players were even suspended.[4]

While he was a member of the Los Angeles Lakers, Nick Van Exel got into an argument with referee Ron Garretson in a game against the Denver Nuggets. Unable to control his temper, Van Exel pushed the referee into the scorer's table. Although Van Exel received a seven-game suspension for his actions, many league officials felt that his punishment was not severe enough.[5]

Perhaps the most highly publicized of all the current professional basketball players is Dennis Rodman of the Chicago Bulls. Between 1992 and 1997, Rodman had been involved in fifteen incidents in which he was either fined, suspended, or both for violating league rules. His list of infractions includes fighting, head-butting other players, arguing with officials and other players, verbally abusing referees, and even kicking a sidelines television photographer in the groin. Rodman was required to pay more than one hundred thousand dollars in fines and has lost more than one million dollars in pay as a result of his accumulated suspensions.[6]

Despite his reputation and the negative media attention, Rodman is still very much a crowd favorite. If it felt Rodman was a danger to the game, the NBA could suspend him indefinitely. However, Rodman sells tickets, and his brand of basketball seems to be what many fans are paying to see.

Fighting on the Ice

Ice hockey has one of the worst reputations for being rough. The National Hockey League has estimated that each season, on the average, five thousand stitches are sewn into its players. It is not uncommon for a single player to receive four hundred stitches over the course of his career.[7]

However, fighting has not always been a part of ice hockey. Fights are rarely seen at the college level or at Olympic hockey games. At the professional level, however, the on-the-ice fights sell tickets, and to some team owners, that is the most important overall consideration.

Many ice hockey fans will confess that one of the reasons they go to the games is to see the hockey players fight. During the early 1970s, the Philadelphia Flyers rewrote the rules of the game to include nightly brawls. Featuring such local heroes as Dave "the Hammer" Schultz and Bob "the Hound" Kelly, the Flyers developed a reputation as the bad boys of the game and were lovingly christened the "Broad Street Bullies" by their fans. In 1974 and 1975, they won the league championship, known as the Stanley Cup. As a result of the Flyers' violent behavior on the ice, several of the league's rules regarding fighting and penalties were changed. However, fighting is still very much a part of the game. According to Jody MacDonald, a Philadelphia sportscaster on a popular all-sports radio show, the NHL could stop the fighting at any time simply by enforcing its rules. However, team owners and league officials recognize the truth that it is the colorful brawls that bring many of their fans to the games.

In the minor leagues, too, Philadelphia seems to have a monopoly on hockey brawlers. The Philadelphia Phantoms are a minor-league team that began its first season in 1996. By far, the most popular player on the team is Frank "the Animal" Bialowas. He knows that he is a role player and was not hired to score goals. Bialowas earned the nickname several years ago when he played for Roanoke in the East Coast Hockey League. "The Animal" is five feet eleven inches and weighs two hundred thirty pounds. His primary role, when he is on the ice, seems to be causing mayhem and starting fights. Delirious fans chant "we want Frank" at every home game.

Although some fights have led to serious injuries and even to the arrest of players after a game, they have not, until very recently, been seriously curtailed. Clarence Campbell, one-time president of the National Hockey League, called the fighting, "A well-established safety valve for the players." Campbell added, "If violence ceases to exist, it [hockey] will not be the same game. Insofar as fighting is part of the show, certainly, we sell it. We do not promote it. We tolerate it, and bring it under disciplinary control which we believe satisfies the public."[8]

Although during recent years violent outbursts have been on the rise in both basketball and baseball, the NHL has actually taken some steps to curb the fighting in its league. After the 1986–1987 season, new regulations and guidelines were put into effect.

The key part of these new rules threatened that any player who left the bench to join in a fight would receive a ten-game suspension without pay. The coach, too, would be suspended for five games if he participated. Although this rule change has not eliminated fighting altogether, it has helped decrease the number of bench-clearing brawls.[9]

Violence in the Ring

Boxing, a sport whose main objective is for one man (or woman) to knock his (or her) opponent unconscious, has had its share of brutality. Although

Although hockey does not have to be violent, often it is. The Philadelphia Flyers, shown here, are well known for participating in fights with their opponents.

the sport has managed to survive since the days of the ancient Greeks, it is only in recent years that the degree of brutality involved in boxing has been widely publicized.

On September 28, 1997, in Las Vegas, Nevada, John Montantes died from injuries sustained in a fight with James Crayton. Although the fight was stopped in the sixth round, the tragic damage had already been done. Montantes was the third professional fighter in three years to die from boxing injuries. His death was only one of more than five hundred attributed to boxing matches since the turn of the century.[10]

One of the most gruesome and shocking acts in boxing history took place in June 1997. In the third round of a heavyweight title bout in Las Vegas between challenger Mike Tyson and champion Evander Holyfield, Tyson savagely bit off a piece of Holyfield's ear. The bout was stopped, Tyson was disqualified, and Holyfield was taken to a nearby hospital to have the cartilage of his ear repaired.[11] After a hearing, the Nevada State Athletic Commission suspended Tyson's boxing license and fined him $3 million.

In contrast to this instant brutalization, sometimes the effects of boxing injuries take many years to surface. Boxing legend Muhammad Ali held the title of World Heavyweight Champion from 1964 to 1967 and again from 1974 to 1978. Today, Ali suffers from an ailment known as Parkinson's syndrome. This defect is caused by the brain's inability to produce a chemical called dopamine

Mike Tyson (right) pushes Evander Holyfield in their infamous heavyweight boxing match on June 26, 1997.

needed to regulate normal brain activity. In Ali's case, the defect was accelerated by the repeated pounding to his head over the course of many boxing matches that had taken place over the years. Although Ali's condition is currently stabilized, he continues to experience mental problems, tremors, and muscle weakness.[12]

In response to the great number of deaths and injuries caused by boxing matches, the American Medical Association (AMA) began issuing editorials criticizing the sport of boxing and even tried to get it

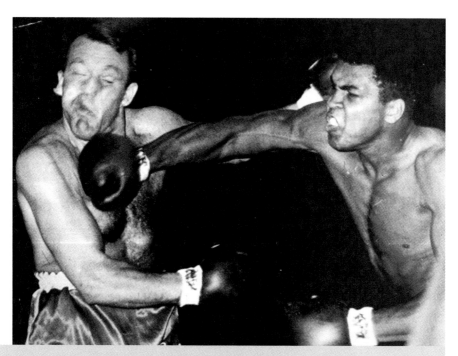

Brian London's face shows the impact of a blow from Muhammed Ali (right) in a heavyweight title boxing match on August 6, 1966.

banned. In its report, which appeared in the January 14, 1983 edition of the *Journal of the American Medical Association (JAMA)*, the AMA revealed that as many as 15 percent of professional boxers suffered brain damage each year. This number translates into between eighteen hundred and forty-five hundred injuries overall. The AMA report concluded that "boxing is a dangerous sport and can result in death or long-term brain injury."[13]

Problems in Baseball

Even the great "national pastime," the all-American game of baseball, long considered the model of wholesome family entertainment, has not escaped the trend toward on-the-field violence. Several incidents in recent years have raised the concern of the league as well as the interest level of the fans. The game has become downright dangerous.

In July 1987, during a game between the Chicago Cubs and the San Diego Padres, Padre pitcher Eric Show hit Cub batter Andre Dawson in the head with a ninety-mile-an-hour fastball. Dawson required twenty-four stitches to close the gash on his cheek. Immediately after the incident, players from both teams charged out from their respective dugouts onto the field, and a major brawl broke out. This was not the first time a pitcher had hit a batter in the head.

Fortunately, only one player has ever died from a head injury inflicted during a baseball game. In 1920, in the days before batters were required to wear helmets, Ray Chapman of the Cleveland Indians was struck in the head by a pitch from Carl Mays of the New York Yankees. Chapman died as a result of his injury.[14]

Umpires, as well as opposing players, have also been on the receiving end of some players' hostilities. An umpire's job is becoming increasingly confrontational. Although for years fans have been aware that officials contend with verbal abuse and with players kicking dirt at them on a regular basis, no one was ready for what happened in 1996. During a disagreement in a game between the Baltimore Orioles and the Toronto Blue Jays, Oriole

Here the Pittsburgh Pirates and the Chicago Cubs indulge in a bench-clearing brawl during the 1993 major-league baseball season.

player Roberto Alomar spit in the face of home-plate umpire John Hirschbeck. Although Alomar was ejected from the game and suspended, he was still allowed to play in the all-important postseason games. This decision by league officials almost caused the umpires to go out on strike in protest to the league's leniency toward Alomar. Even though Alomar's infraction did not technically constitute actual physical violence, his action clearly demonstrated a severe lack of respect for order, authority, and good sportsmanship.

4

Sports Violence and Young People

Sadly, acts of sports violence have not been limited to the professional fields, courts, and rinks. Incidents have begun to trickle down to the college and even the high school levels. Here, too, the types of violence can be sorted into the same two basic categories as in professional sports. One type of violence is a built-in part of the game. Rough physical contact can cause debilitating and sometimes life-threatening injuries. The other type of violence is the result of "extracurricular," or off-the-field, fighting and brutality.

34

Early Sports Programs

In the United States, the establishment of youth sports programs was designed to give young boys, and later, girls, the opportunity to play organized sports in a safe, controlled environment under careful adult supervision. The goal of such programs was to promote athletic achievement as well as good sportsmanship.

Little League Baseball was founded in 1939 in Williamsport, Pennsylvania, by Carl Stotz, a local merchant. The purpose of the program was to develop the qualities of "citizenship, discipline, teamwork and physical well-being." According to the

Competitive sports like baseball can be a healthy activity for high school players.

program's agenda in *The Mission and Management of Little League Baseball*: "By espousing the virtues of character, courage, and loyalty, the Little League Baseball program is designed to develop superior citizens rather than superior athletes."[1]

From its modest beginnings as one sole league in a small upstate Pennsylvania town, the Little League program has grown worldwide. It now features more than twenty-seven thousand teams made up of nine-year-olds to twelve-year-olds of both genders. Additional programs have been added to include older youths, ranging up to eighteen years old. A softball program and a challenge division for mentally and physically handicapped children have also been added.

Youth football also developed a program whose ideals were to mix academics and athletics. It was begun in 1929 by Glenn Scobie "Pop" Warner. According to *Pop Warner's Official Rules*, the program was established to "inspire youth, regardless of race, creed, or national origin, to practice the ideals of sportsmanship, scholarship and physical fitness."[2] The program now extends from the "mitey mites," ages seven to nine, to the "bantam" level of play for teens aged thirteen to fifteen.

Many young athletes get their sports training in school. Many middle schools, junior highs, and high schools have extensive athletic programs in which students play teams from other schools. Many coaches double as teachers at some schools, but others are hired for the specific purpose of coaching a sports team.

Youth football programs now include divisions like "mighty mites," for ages seven to nine, through "bantams," for ages thirteen to fifteen.

At the high school level there are district and state championships, especially in football and basketball. The games are often played in neutral-territory stadiums that can hold thousands of spectators. These crowds contribute additional monies toward the participating schools, which use the funds collected as admission fees to enhance their athletic programs. Sometimes a team has to travel long distances, often at great expense to the school, to participate in regional and state playoff games. The importance placed on these games can create tremendous stress on young athletes.

An example can be found in H.G. Bissinger's

book, *Friday Night Lights*, which highlights the story of the Odessa, Texas, Permian High School football team, the Panthers, and its quest to be the best high school football team in the state. Much of the social activity of the town centered on the players, the cheerleaders, and the coaches. The author reveals that on Friday nights as many as twenty thousand fans would flock to the stadium to see a game.

Violent Injuries

In sports, most violence is caused by circumstances that are simply part of the game. In fact, most game-related injuries result from the regular demands of the sport and not from any illegal action. For example, during the 1987 high school and college football season, it was reported that four players died and more than three hundred thousand were injured playing football. In addition, on the average, more than thirty college and high school students are paralyzed each year as a result of football injuries.[3]

Violent injuries during school sporting events are not as rare as most people believe. A study was conducted by Dr. Barry Maron for *The New England Journal of Medicine* regarding sports trauma injuries. In the cases studied, involving the death of twenty-five young people between 1977 and 1995, Maron learned that death was caused by an unexpected blow to the chest. Sixteen of these deaths occurred in the sport of baseball; two in softball; four in ice hockey; and one each in football, karate, and lacrosse.[4]

Many fatal sports injuries also result from injuries to the head. In August 1996, Justin Rutland, a thirteen-year-old soccer player from Pennsylvania, died five days after playing in a tournament in which he "headed" (hit the ball with his head) a soccer ball. The impact of the ball had caused his brain to hemorrhage, or bleed internally, which eventually led to his death.[5] The header was a regular type of soccer game play, not an accident.

Second-impact syndrome or postconcussion syndrome, like the type suffered by running back Merril Hoge, is another serious type of head injury. This syndrome, or group of symptoms, is generally related to the game of football. It is caused by repeated blows to the head and can often result in concussions and swelling in the brain. Sometimes it can lead to death. Such was the case with high school student Adrian Guitterez.

Guitterez was a running back for the Monte Vista, Colorado, football team. In 1991, Guitterez suffered a slight concussion during a game. Later, he complained of a slight headache and soreness. He thought he had a cold. Two weeks later, in a game against Alamosa, Guitterez was tackled hard, got up, and then collapsed. Guitterez died five days later.[6]

Marc Buoniconti, the son of former NFL player Nick Buoniconti, suffered a severe injury in a game. Marc played college football for the Citadel. On October 26, 1985, in a game against East Tennessee State University, Buoniconti tackled running back Herman Jacob. The impact from the play severely damaged Marc's spinal cord, and he was left paralyzed in both arms and legs, thus ending his college playing career and dramatically changing his life forever. Buoniconti is still confined to a wheelchair.[7]

Injuries from Fighting

Pressure for athletes to win at all costs is growing. Winning in high school can lead to college scholarships. Winning in college sports can lead to multimillion-dollar contracts to play at the professional level. Success at the professional level can lead to fame and celebrity status and even to bigger guaranteed salaries and revenue from product endorsements. All this emphasis on winning and on making money has led to an increase in violent behavior by athletes.

During the fall of 1996, the soccer teams of Pinelands Regional High School and Manchester Township High School, both in New Jersey, were involved in a close match. With less than two minutes left in the game, a fight broke out between two players, one from each team. Soon other players jumped into the fight. One Manchester player suffered a concussion from having been kicked in the head and required stitches. During the ride home, the Pinelands school bus carrying their team was stopped by the local police, and two players on the bus were arrested for having kicked the Manchester player and charged with aggravated assault. They were kept overnight in a juvenile detention facility and released the following day after a hearing. The next day, the parents of the Pinelands students filed countercharges against the Manchester players involved in the affair. In this incident, members of both high school teams had turned an athletic contest into a personal brawl.[8]

In January 1997, an incident took place in Philadelphia that further highlights how young athletes, trying to act like their professional role models, have endangered high school scholastic sports. Larry Nicholson, a seventeen-year-old, six-feet four-inch-tall high school senior played basketball for Murrell Dobbins Technical High School. He had been wanting to win a high school league championship for a very long time. It looked as if 1997 could be the year, but something got in the way. At a Philadelphia Public League game, upset over a call that the referee had made, Nicholson punched the referee in the face. Nicholson was then arrested by the police and taken from the game in handcuffs. The referee, Ron Palmer, was taken to a local hospital, where he was treated for a bloody nose and given six stitches under his eye. Palmer decided to press charges, and, as a result, Nicholson was charged with simple and aggravated assault, and reckless endangerment. He also received a five-day suspension from school.

Rich Yankowitz, the coach of Nicholson's team, commented, ". . . one thing is for certain: his [Nicholson's] high school athletic career is over."[9] As far as anyone could remember, this was the first time any Philadelphia player had punched an official.

In a follow-up editorial in the sports section of *The Philadelphia Inquirer*, columnist Bill Lyon said:

> The easiest, most obviously direct link, the one that all the pop psychologists want to make, is a straight line, Dennis Rodman to Larry Nicholson. . . . Much of what Rodman . . . does is premeditated and shrewdly calculated to call attention to himself. His banker can tell you how well this pays.[10]

Adults and students alike must wonder: What is the message that our professional athletes are sending to athletes still in school? Many suspect that the main message is that if you are a sports superstar, a different set of rules will apply to you.

When interviewed, one former college hockey player said that he had not originally been a "go and kill 'em" type of player. However, after having been punched at center ice on numerous occasions, having had his helmet ripped off his head by the stick of an opposing player, and having frequently exchanged punches, he, too, had become, a "go and kill 'em" hockey player, in "self-defense."[11]

Parents' Involvement

It's not only the students in school sports who need to examine their personal goals and standards. Many parents are to blame for the aggression in youth sports programs. Moms and dads can also get caught up in the frenzy of the game and in the notion that winning is all that matters. In the pursuit of winning, some parents have resorted to cheating and deceit. In Chesapeake, Virginia, for example, the Deep Creek Redskins junior football team had to forfeit all its games, and a chance to win the championship, because one team member turned out to be over age. The boy's mother was subsequently questioned about whether she intentionally put the wrong birthdate on her son's application.[12]

Many Little League Baseball organizers have also complained about problems with parents. One league commissioner instructed the umpires to stop any game in which parents got out of hand. On some occasions, the local police had to be called when parents got carried away. These actions set the wrong example for their children.[13] According to Robert Yeager in his book, *Seasons of Shame*:

> Parents scream into the faces of coaches and referees, hand out diet pills and plastic suits to their overweight kids, sock it out over close calls, or yell about whether their offspring should play shortstop or second base. In Livermore, California, abusive remarks and threats from parents and fans prompted so many referees to quit that the president of the local referees association warned that the entire program was endangered.[14]

Coaches' Behavior

Coaches, too, can get caught up in the intensity of the game and take out their own aggressions on the players, particularly in college athletics. Perhaps one of the most notorious misdeeds by a coach occurred during the 1978 Gator Bowl game between the Ohio State University and Clemson football teams. After an interception by Clemson that just about sealed a loss for Ohio State, longtime Ohio State head coach Wayne Woodrow "Woody" Hayes slugged the

Clemson player who made the interception, Charlie Bauman, three times after trying to help him up from the sidelines. This incident took place in full view of a packed stadium and a national television audience. Hayes was fired the next day for this inexcusable act and ungloriously ended what had previously been a distinguished career as a coach.[15]

In another incident that made the national news, Indiana University basketball coach Bobby Knight, who has a history of violent outbursts toward his players and officials, threw a chair across the court during a game.

For two consecutive games during the 1987 college basketball season, the Cornell University team had been involved in fights. One occurred on December 7, 1987, in a game against Syracuse University. Cornell's Greg Gilda and Syracuse's Derrick Brower were pushing each other under the basket. Punches were thrown, and both players were ejected from the game.[16]

In 1988, a meeting of the Big East Conference executive committee was called by then basketball commissioner Dave Gavitt to discuss the increase in the number of fights occurring on the court during college basketball games. The issues the executive committee discussed are still valid today.

College basketball had changed gradually over the twenty years preceding this meeting. Student athletes were becoming faster and stronger, and many coaches had raised the tempo of the game to take advantage of this new type of faster, stronger player. Pressure from the coaches contributed to the risk of

Bobby Knight, longtime basketball coach at Indiana University, has a substantial record of violent outbursts.

violent behavior on the court by the athletes. The motivation to win at all costs creates intense pressure to succeed on everyone involved.

At the conference executive committee meeting, many coaches expressed the feeling that sloppy officiating had also caused problems. Referees had called games differently during the regular season than they had during the playoffs; officials had let some violations slide during playoffs that they would otherwise have called fouls during the regular season. Coaches felt that the game should be decided by the teams on the field, not by the officials.

An explanation for the change in the nature of college basketball games was offered by Art Hyland, supervisor of officials for the Big East Conference: "The pot at the end of the rainbow is bigger. If you're good, you got a chance to be looked at and get a pro contract."[17] With more at stake, student athletes play more aggressively to impress both the pro scouts and the coaches.

Some Unusual Eruptions of Violence

Even college mascots have been involved in outbreaks of violence. In February 1995, during a basketball game between Stanford University and the University of California at Berkeley, Stanford's mascot, a seven-foot-tall pine tree, got into a wrestling match with California's Golden Bear. Both of the mascots were taken from the game by police.

In January 1988, in Philadelphia, three male LaSalle College cheerleaders started a fight when they tried to prevent the mascot of rival St. Joseph's University, a hawk, from flapping his wings.

Even the marching bands of opposing teams have gotten involved in the frenzy of college football. On September 19, 1998, during a game between Prairie View A & M University and Southern University, a fight broke out between members of the two bands. According to George Edwards, Prairie View's band director, the estimated damage to band instruments totaled about twenty thousand dollars.[18]

Although the uniforms (or costumes) may be different from the players', the message is the same: Inappropriately aggressive behavior or taunting at sporting events will be tolerated because that's what the spectators seem to enjoy.

With acts of violence breaking out routinely on rinks, fields, and courts, it is not surprising that eventually it would spill over into the stadiums and even into the streets. In the United States, as well as in many other countries, spectator violence has been steadily on the rise.

5

Fan Violence

Participating athletes, coaches, sports officials, mascots, and marching bands are not the only parties to get involved in violent acts. Spectators are also getting caught up in the emotions of the game. Several years ago, one of the most bizarre incidents in sports sharply illustrated the growing problem of violence by spectators at sporting events. The incident did not happen at a prizefight or at a hockey game. It happened at a match in the traditionally well-bred sport of women's professional tennis.

48

Violence in the Stands

In May 1993, nineteen-year-old tennis star Monica Seles was competing at the Rothenbaum Tennis Club in Hamburg, Germany, in the Citizen Cup Tennis Tournament. Her opponent was Magdalena Maleeva of Bulgaria. During a brief break between games, in plain view of hundreds of spectators, a man rushed from the stands onto the court and stabbed Seles in the left shoulder with a nine-inch knife. The attacker, a thirty-eight-year-old unemployed German machine operator, named Gunter Parche, was grabbed first by a spectator, then by security guards, and was later arrested. He was charged with attempted murder. When Parche was questioned by the police about his motives, he confessed that the reason he stabbed Seles was to prevent her from taking away the number-one-ranked women's tennis position from Germany's star player, Steffi Graf. Parche was convicted and received a two-year suspended sentence from a German court.[1]

Prior to this incident, which occurred during the war in Bosnia, Seles had received several death threats because of her Serbian heritage. These threats appeared to be unrelated to the assault on her at the tennis match. The Women's Tennis Association agreed to step up security at future tennis matches, but as one official said, "How can you provide 100 percent protection? You can't."[2] After more than a year away from the sport, Monica Seles returned to tennis competition. Still, she has yet to achieve the level of success she had known before the stabbing.

At regular-season professional football games, violent acts among spectators have also become a concern. During one game in 1994 between the Los Angeles Raiders and the Los Angeles Rams, police arrested fourteen people, removed fifty-five others from the stadium, and broke up at least twenty-five other incidents. According to Thomas Bassler, a Rams fan, the fights were often the best part of attending the game.[3]

During the 1997 professional football season, the Philadelphia Eagles, concerned about fan violence in the stands, agreed with the Philadelphia city

In 1993, Monica Seles was taken out of professional tennis for many months by a knife-wielding spectator at a tournament in Hamburg, Germany.

government to place a magistrate at all home games. Offenders were quickly taken by police to a makeshift court set up right in the stadium, where fines or arrests could be imposed on the spot. Although only a few people were actually arrested, the message came across that fan violence would not be tolerated.

Another violent spectator scene occurred in New York City on July 11, 1996, during a heavyweight boxing match between Riddick Bowe and Andrew Golota in Madison Square Garden. In the seventh round, referee Wayne Kelly stopped the fight and disqualified Golota, who had been winning the fight, for having dealt illegal, low blows. Bowe was lying on the floor of the ring in great pain. Within seconds, dozens of onlookers jumped into the ring and began exchanging punches. Other spectators began throwing folding chairs and ice into the ring. Golota was hit in the back of the head with a heavy object. The fighting continued and spread into the stands. People were getting trampled, and some had to be taken to local hospitals. According to reports in the *New York Daily News*, ten people were arrested and at least fourteen were hurt. The police were slow to get to the scene, and there were not enough security guards on hand to be able to control the riot.

One spectator commented that he thought the fight was worth the drive up from Washington, D.C.: "We got a little extra. We got about twenty fights for the price of one."[4]

Violent College Fans

On a Saturday in November 1993, a crowd of 77,745 students, parents, and fans came to see the University of Wisconsin football team play the University of Michigan's. Wisconsin won the game for the first time in thirty-one years by a score of 13–10, earning its team the Big Ten Conference championship and a trip to the annual Rose Bowl game in Pasadena, California. As the game ended, the enthusiastic crowd stormed onto the field. In the process, they knocked down two fences. In the mad rush that followed, seventy-three people were injured, six of them critically. The playing field soon became cluttered with ambulances, paramedics, and players who were trying to assist the injured spectators. Although the police had added extra officers to help patrol the crowds, many of them said they were unprepared to deal with the crush that occurred following the game.[5]

Although this event gained national attention, it was not the first sports-related problem at the University of Wisconsin. During the eighties, there had been many incidents of drinking, shooting slingshots, and hoisting fellow spectators and passing them from one section of the stadium to another. As a result of this disruptive behavior, the director of security introduced some security measures. These included frisking fans (to see whether they were hiding alcoholic beverages), using video-monitoring cameras, and issuing summonses. He said, "When police routinely remove, on average, more than a hundred persons from the stadium during each home game, something is obviously wrong."[6]

Columbus, Ohio, is another city with a high-profile college football team. On September 29, 1996, after the Ohio State Buckeyes soundly defeated Notre Dame, a crowd of Ohio State fans set fire to several trash containers, threw rocks, and overturned cars. The local police reported that five people were arrested for minor offenses. About twenty to thirty police officers were needed to break up a crowd of several hundred people. It even became necessary to use chemical spray to get the crowd to leave the area.[7]

High School Problems

Unfortunately, spectator violence has also trickled down to the high school level. During the fourth quarter of a girls' basketball game between Franklin Learning Center and Central High School in Philadelphia, a fight broke out in the stands. Police had to remove two males who were not associated with either school. Several students, as well as adult spectators, received minor injuries. The game was resumed after a twenty-minute delay, and the only spectators allowed to remain were the players' family members and the faculty from both participating schools. This was the first reported violent incident at a girls' basketball game. However, in 1991, South Philadelphia High School had to close several of its boys' basketball games to the general public because of postgame fights.[8]

In March 1997, a high school playoff basketball game between Atlantic City High School and Camden High School in New Jersey was called before time was up because fumes from pepper gas spray began to filter into the gym where the game was being played. Police had used the spray to break up a disturbance that was taking place outside, behind the gym. The Camden High School athletic director had been struck in the head with a stone. One Atlantic City High School student developed breathing problems from the fumes of the spray. Another student was beaten in the parking lot after the game and had to be taken to a local hospital for treatment of facial and head injuries. No arrests were made.[9]

One of the most brutal high school incidents took place in a suburb of Kansas City, Missouri. A seventeen-year-old senior at Shawnee Mission North High School was charged with two counts of murder in the shooting deaths of a fifteen-year-old sophomore and a nineteen-year-old student from a rival high school. The incident occurred during the weekend after a hotly contested football game between Shawnee Mission and Olathe North High schools. Taunting and insults during the game had led to a fistfight in the stands, during which two teens were ultimately arrested for drunken and disorderly conduct. The incident then carried over from Friday night to Sunday, when students from both schools met in a parking lot. The student accused of murder allegedly fired shots from a semiautomatic handgun. Aside from the two murder victims, four other people were injured.[10]

Fan violence at high school sporting events can become deadly when guns are brought to games.

Postgame Violence

Pick up a local newspaper after a professional championship game and you may read about postgame looting and riots in the streets in addition to learning about the final score or the heroes of the game. Millions of dollars' worth of property damage, numerous injuries to innocent people, and even several deaths have resulted from postgame riots. Chicago and Detroit are only two of many cities that have had their championship images tarnished by violent postgame celebrations.

In 1968, the Detroit Tigers won the World Series. In the city's celebration that followed the Tigers' victory, numerous windows were broken, one woman was raped, and more than two hundred arrests were made. This was just the first of many professional sports incidents involving fans who lost control and caused damage to property and injury to innocent bystanders. It was an indication that simply winning a championship was not enough to satisfy a hometown crowd. In recent years, city governments have been forced to spend millions of dollars to hire extra police and security personnel to control the crowds and clean up the streets after victory celebrations and parades.

The Chicago sports fans have a particularly poor record for celebrating their sports teams' successes. In June 1992, the Chicago Bulls won their second NBA championship. During the victory celebration, one thousand people were arrested, one hundred were injured, and sixty-one police cars were damaged. Several stores were completely destroyed by the looting and fires that followed. The price tag for the damages totaled more than $10 million.

One year later, on June 20, 1993, when the Bulls won the NBA championship for a third time, the situation did not improve, even though Chicago had spent about $3 million for police and fire protection to help limit possible damages by the crowd.[11] Although the actual dollar amount of property damages was significantly lower than it had been in the previous year, three people were killed, including a twelve-year-old boy, in the atmosphere of mayhem that followed the end of the game.

According to a report in *Sports Illustrated* magazine, when the Detroit Pistons won the NBA championship in 1990, the fans' reaction was brutal. Seven deaths were reported, and hundreds of people were injured. There were also numerous reports of shootings, stabbings, and fights. Among those killed were four children who died in two separate auto accidents when celebrants drove their cars onto a crowded sidewalk.[12]

Fan violence has been widespread and not limited to merely one or two sports. Violent events occurred after teams won the World Series, the Super Bowl, and the Stanley Cup. On the night of June 9, 1993, the Montreal Canadiens defeated the Los Angeles Kings to win the Stanley Cup. A crowd gathered on St. Catherine Street outside Montreal's hockey arena, the Forum. Large groups of mostly young men came ready to loot and destroy. They were armed with bricks and had bags for hauling away goods. They overwhelmed the six hundred regular policemen and specially trained riot squads that had been sent downtown to maintain order. As a result, $10 million of merchandise was looted from downtown Montreal stores. Forty-seven police cars were also damaged. Reports indicated that 168 people were injured and 115 arrested.[13] In June 1996, in Denver, when the Colorado Avalanche won the Stanley Cup for the first time, similar incidents of vandalism were reported.

Thanks to a plea for calm from public officials and a strong police presence, history did not repeat itself in 1997, and the city of Detroit managed not to live up to its former, out-of-control reputation. In June of that year, the NHL's Detroit Red Wings won the Stanley Cup for the first time in forty-two years. A parade was held downtown to celebrate the victory. According to an interview with sports columnist Bob Wojnowski of *The Detroit News*, more than one million people attended the parade, and by all accounts, there was no violence, no looting, and only one arrest. Detroit's experience showed that with thoughtful planning, it is possible for fans to rejoice and celebrate a championship without turning a town into a war zone.

Fan Violence in Other Countries

Fan violence is not unique to the United States. It has also been notable in Great Britain, and the loyal British soccer fans have even exported their particular type of violence to other countries.

Gangs of "hooligans" routinely ferry across the English Channel to attend soccer matches in other European countries. These rowdy fans have gotten drunk, terrorized the towns, and stirred up fights at various soccer stadiums. In May 1985, Heysel Stadium in Brussels, Belgium, was the site of the European Cup soccer championships. During a game between Liverpool (England) and Juventus (Italy), a riot broke out in the stands. Thirty-nine spectators, mostly Italians, were killed. Another four hundred people were injured.[14] The law-abiding fans of the game, as well as the players, had been made to suffer at the hands of a small but intimidating minority. As a result of these and other riots, the Union of European Football Associations (UEFA) voted to ban all English soccer clubs from competing anywhere in Europe for a period of five years. In addition, many pubs in Great Britain refuse to allow their patrons to wear soccer team colors, for fear of promoting fighting in their establishments among fans of different teams.

Soccer, also popular in Central and South America, has been the catalyst for incidents of violent spectator outbursts there as well. When the Brazilian soccer team won the World Cup soccer tournament in 1970, more than 2 million people went to the streets to celebrate the victory. As a result of this celebration, more than forty people died and eighteen hundred were injured.[15]

The Role of the Media

With the creation of cable and satellite television and the development of all-sports television networks like ESPN and Fox Sports, more and more viewers have access to an increasingly wide variety of sporting events. These include high school, college, and professional sports. The use of instant replays on videotape means that a particularly violent event can be shown again and again. These violent acts seem to be replayed on television as often as the great plays of the game.

Many critics have accused the media of contributing to the increase in incidents of sports

The sign on this pub door in Great Britain shows the measures the owner has taken to avoid violent encounters over sporting events in his bar. Europeans call soccer "football."

violence at the nonprofessional level. In an article that appeared in *The New York Times* in February 1988, columnist Peter Alfano pointed out that although the media is able to downplay or ignore violent outbursts, they usually choose not to. Alfano's position, in fact, was that some journalists even try to glorify the violence to sell more newspapers.

In response to these accusations, Mike Matters, a coordinating producer for ESPN's "Sportscenter" said: "We hope that we don't put clips [of violence] on just for the sake of it. We're not trying to glamorize what the players are doing. Our anchor people have been outspoken about fighting."[16]

Why the Violent Behavior from Fans?

Sociologist Irving Goldaber said,

> Fans aren't just interested in winning games anymore . . . they have to vanquish the other team. When people come into the stands, they begin to feel the power to affect the outcome of the game. Now there is the feeling they can do something to help. America is a candidate for a new kind of violence—the fans' desire to achieve power vicariously.[17]

Some research has indicated that the aggressive actions of fans may be related to their hormone levels. A research study, conducted at Georgia State University in 1996, tested male students before and after they watched certain sporting events. The study showed that the men's levels of testosterone (a male hormone related to aggressive tendencies) increased sharply after their favorite team won and decreased when it lost.[18]

Critics of sports violence also point an accusing finger at the liquor and beer sold at and brought to sporting events. One college police officer said that "males on booze are the main contributors to fights. Women aren't the problem. It's men between [the ages of] sixteen and twenty-six on booze, drugs, or showing off to impress girls."[19]

In one study commissioned by major-league baseball, it was reported that 77 percent of the violent fights taking place in baseball stadiums occurred in the least expensive seats, and that many of these incidents took place during the late innings of a game after the fans had plenty of time to drink alcoholic beverages.[20]

As a result, many stadiums have either switched to selling low-alcohol beer or have limited the hours in which alcoholic beverages are sold during games. It is ironic to note that the Montreal Canadiens hockey team is owned by the Molson Brewing Company of Canada, which sells its products at all of the Canadien hockey games.

In many small cities and towns across the United States there are minor-league teams. These leagues charge lower admission fees, and their games are more family-oriented and less violent. There are several reasons why this low-key approach is possible. First, players in the minor leagues do not receive big salaries. They are playing for the love of the game and to impress scouts from the majors.

They do not have a national following of fans, nor do they earn product endorsements. Second, because one goal of the minor-league teams is to develop a family following, many of their stadiums refuse to sell alcoholic beverages. Banning alcohol helps eliminate the problem of rowdy fans.

Critics of sports violence point to liquor and beer sold at or brought to sporting events as a contributing factor.

6

Violence Off the Field

Sports fans follow the actions of their favorite professional athletes not only on the field but off the field as well. Sometimes, players' behavior off the field subjects them to criticism. Once, while he was a player for the Phoenix Suns, basketball star Charles Barkley spit in the face of a young fan. After the incident, Barkley was severely criticized by the media for displaying behavior that was "unbecoming to a role model." However, on several occasions, Barkley protested to the media that he never claimed to be a role model for young people.[1]

Despite Barkley's comments and viewpoint, the fact is that professional athletes are role models for many of our young people today. Each year, sports fans spend millions of dollars on team logo merchandise like jackets, hats, sneakers, and sports drinks because a particular product is being promoted by a favorite athlete. Crowds of loyal followers routinely wait in long lines to get autographs, photos, and other mementos of their favorite players. More important, kids actually pattern their lives after the athletes they idolize.

The Cowboys' Record

In the category of most off-the-field scandals, the Dallas Cowboys may currently hold the lead. Although the team has been proclaimed "America's Team" by the media and has enjoyed a great following across the United States, several Cowboy players have been involved in dangerous and illegal activities. According to a story that appeared in *Newsweek* magazine in April 1995, Erik Williams, a twenty-eight-year-old all-pro offensive tackle, was accused of sexually assaulting a seventeen-year-old girl. The case was settled out of court, and Williams was not indicted. He had previously been serving a two-year term of probation stemming from a drunk driving charge, and subsequently he served a term of probation resulting from drug charges.[2]

In 1996, another one of the team's superstars, Michael Irvin, received a four-year term consisting of court probation as well as a five-game suspension for possession of illegal drugs.[3]

Even the Cowboys' coach was plagued by legal problems: During the summer of 1997, Barry Switzer, former head coach, was arrested at the Dallas-Fort Worth Airport for carrying a loaded gun. He was fined $75,000 by team owner Jerry Jones.[4]

After several seasons during which personal problems greatly damaged the image and reputation of the team, the Cowboys hired Calvin Hill, one of their former star players, along with his wife, to run a program to help improve players' behavior. Hill's program, started in Dallas in 1997, still includes an orientation meeting for new players, as well as informational sessions on security and spirituality. Previously, Hill had been credited with starting a program in Cleveland, Ohio, known as the Inner Circle, the first drug rehabilitation program run by an NFL team.[5]

Off-the-field violence by professional athletes is certainly not limited to one team. In 1973, former Pittsburgh Steelers defensive tackle Ernie Holmes went on a shooting rampage in eastern Ohio. According to a story in *Sports Illustrated*, after an unsuccessful attempt to reconcile with his first wife, Holmes began shooting at a truck with both a pistol and a shotgun. During the subsequent police chase, Holmes shot and wounded a police helicopter pilot before he was finally caught. Holmes pleaded guilty to a charge of assault with a deadly weapon. He was placed on probation for five years and spent two

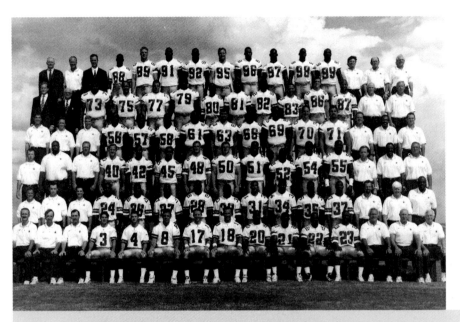

The Dallas Cowboys have affectionately been known as "America's Team," but they have had problems with the off-field behavior of some players. This photo shows the Cowboys' 1997 team.

months in a psychiatric hospital in Pittsburgh, Pennsylvania.[6]

In October 1997, during a bar brawl in Orlando, Florida, Charles Barkley, then with the NBA's Houston Rockets, was charged with battery, disorderly conduct, criminal mischief, and resisting arrest. Barkley was accused of throwing another bar patron through a window. He claimed that he had been provoked by the man, who allegedly threw a glass of ice at a table where Barkley was seated. An out-of-court settlement was reached with the victim.[7]

College Outlaws

College players who look up to the professionals have also been involved in off-the-field violence. Murray Sperber, professor of English at Indiana University, wrote in his book, *College Sports Inc.*, that there is an unwritten "very important persons law" that gives special treatment and benefits to college athletes, particularly when they get in trouble with the law. In a survey of three hundred fifty schools, a study conducted by *The Philadelphia Daily News* in 1986 showed that from 1983 to 1987, there were at least sixty incidents of sexual assaults perpetrated by college athletes and that "football and basketball players were 38 percent more likely to be implicated than the average male college student."[8]

Tommy Kane played college football at Syracuse University. During the 1987 season, Kane led the National Collegiate Athletic Association (NCAA) in touchdown catches. On a night in April 1988, Kane's car was being ticketed for a parking violation. When the police officer learned that there were nineteen outstanding parking tickets in the owner's name, the car was ordered to be towed away. However, before the tow truck arrived,

> Kane tried to drive away after having closed the door on the policewoman's arm. Other police intervened and arrested Kane, charging him with second degree assault, a felony, and misdemeanor counts of resisting arrest and obstructing governmental administration.[9]

Normally, anyone accused of these charges would

have been held for trial. Then, if convicted, he would be sent to prison. Instead, in Kane's case, he was offered a plea-bargain in which he pled guilty to the minor charge of disorderly conduct and harassment. His punishment was to perform one hundred hours of community service.[10]

Athletes at Virginia Polytechnic Institute and Virginia State University have also run into problems because of their violent behavior. Since November 1995, nineteen current and former football players have been charged by police with numerous offenses, including rape and malicious wounding. In July 1997, Sean Sullivan, who was involved in a brawl, was sentenced to thirty days in jail on charges of assault and battery.[11] As a result of the numerous incidents, the university organized a committee of faculty members and students to discuss the problem. The committee decided to recommended harsher penalties for athletes who break the law. They also suggested developing programs to give more support services to athletes at the university.[12]

At another Virginia institution, Virginia Wesleyan College, twenty-three male athletes were suspended from competition in January 1997, when a fight developed over a woman. The brawl took place at a local bar, then later moved to the college soccer field. Although no students were arrested, two were injured. Eleven baseball, seven basketball, and five lacrosse players were involved. In addition to the suspensions, each player was required to perform twenty-five hours of community service.[13]

Sports and Domestic Violence

According to reports from the Federal Bureau of Investigation (FBI), a woman in this country is beaten by her husband or boyfriend every fifteen seconds. Physical abuse in families is referred to as domestic violence. Unfortunately, athletes are not exceptions to this social problem. Many have been known to abuse their wives or girlfriends. In one of the more highly publicized cases, former heavyweight boxing champion Mike Tyson admitted to beating his ex-wife, Robin Givens, on several occasions. In fact, during an interview, Tyson admitted, "I like to hurt women when I make love to them."[14]

Later, in July 1991, Tyson was indicted for raping a beauty pageant contestant, Desiree Washington, in an Indianapolis hotel room. He was convicted of the assault and served six years of a ten-year prison sentence for his crime.[15]

In May 1998, Riddick Bowe, another professional heavyweight boxer, was arrested in Virginia after kidnapping his former wife and their five children. Bowe was indicted by a federal grand jury on charges of interstate domestic violence to which he pleaded guilty. He was placed under house arrest while awaiting sentencing and was ordered to attend psychological counseling sessions. There are other charges still pending against Bowe.[16]

In one of the most highly publicized court cases of the twentieth century, former college and professional football star O. J. Simpson was tried and acquitted in the murder of his ex-wife, Nicole Brown

Simpson, and her friend Ron Goldman. During the trial, evidence was presented that Nicole had called 911 on several occasions to report having been physically assaulted by her husband. Although Simpson was not convicted in the criminal trial, he did lose a subsequent wrongful death civil suit in 1996 and was ordered to pay more than $30 million in compensation to the families of the two victims.

Basketball stars have also abused their wives or girlfriends. Robert Parish, formerly with the Boston Celtics and then with the Charlotte Hornets, was one of them. His former wife, Nancy Saad, said that on more than one occasion she had been thrown down a flight of stairs by Parish and then kicked as she tried to leave their house in Weston, Massachusetts.[17] In June 1987, the situation got worse.

Saad had gone to Parish's hotel room in Los Angeles right before an NBA playoff game to talk about their son, Justin, and Parish's child-support payments. After a brief shouting match at the door of Parish's hotel room, Saad said that her ex-husband grabbed her by the throat, punched her, and then threw her against a wall in the hallway.[18]

Nancy Saad was taken to Saint John's Hospital and Health Center in Santa Monica, California, where she remained for seven days. Part of her stay was spent in the intensive care unit. Hospital records show that she was diagnosed with "a closed head injury, impaired vision to her right eye, abrasions around her left eye and over her right cheek, a large bruise on her right arm, and soreness and spasms in her neck."[19]

Mark Fitzpatrick was a goaltender for the NHL's Florida Panthers. In July 1994, he shoved and kicked his wife in the back. Susan Fitzpatrick, who was pregnant at the time, contacted the police in Islamorada, Florida, and had her husband arrested. Fitzpatrick was charged with aggravated battery on a pregnant woman and was required to participate in a special program for men who abuse their wives.[20]

Even popular players with otherwise positive reputations have become involved in domestic violence disputes. One such player, Warren Moon, was a star quarterback who played for the Houston Oilers for ten years and later with the NFL's Minnesota Vikings and the Seattle Seahawks. In 1989, he was honored as the NFL's man of the year. In addition to this honor, Moon has been involved in many local fund-raising activities for charities.

In 1995, Moon's seven-year-old son, Jeffrey, dialed 911 to report that his father was beating his mother, Felicia Moon. In Missouri City, Missouri, Mrs. Moon filed a report with the local police department. In that report she claimed that her husband had hit her on the head with his open hand and choked her until she almost passed out.[21] When she managed to break away and leave the house in her car, her husband followed her. Warren Moon finally turned himself in to the Missouri City jail, where he was charged with one count of misdemeanor assault.

He was subsequently released on bail. When asked by the media about the incident, Moon said he felt that it had been blown out of proportion. Later he claimed, "This was not a case of domestic violence, but rather a 'domestic dispute' that had gotten out of hand."[22]

Special Treatment

Because of their elevated status in this country, star athletes often receive special treatment when they get in trouble with the law.

In January 1994, Kansas City Chiefs wide receiver Tim Barnett was released from jail on appeal after receiving a ten-day sentence for his second domestic violence conviction in thirteen months. The release permitted Barnett to play in a critical playoff game. "It tends to send a message that if you've got money, you can manipulate the system. That's not right," said Johnson County, Kansas, district attorney Paul Morrison. "Mr. Barnett needs to be doing his time not because he is a Chief, but because he broke the law."[23]

A similar incident of favoritism occurred involving baseball star Barry Bonds, whose wife took him to court in a dispute over child-support payments. Bonds was asking for a monthly reduction from $15,000 to $7,500 in his child-support payments. The case was heard by Superior Court Judge George Taylor of San Mateo County, California. The judge, a baseball fan, granted the payment reduction and then asked for Bonds's autograph. Two weeks later, after the incident was publicized, Judge Taylor set aside his judgment, returned the autograph, and took himself off the case.[24]

Preferential treatment to athletes also takes place

at the college level. According to a study conducted by *The Washington Post*, it was learned that many athletes' victims, as well as some of the prosecutors involved in legal proceedings, believed that players who committed crimes received special treatment from police and judges.

Joseph Pursch, a medical doctor interviewed by Indiana University professor Murray Sperber, suggested that "because athletes receive preferential treatment from early ages, their social consciences are often underdeveloped." Dr. Pursch offered this scenario for a typical athlete:

> At home he gets away with talking back; in school he gets good grades even when he cuts classes; and his third drunk-driving charge is covered up. . . . And when he gets rough with a cheerleader at two o' clock in the morning, the coach smooths things out with her father.[25]

The Plot Thickens

The bizarre case involving figure skater Tonya Harding during the 1994 United States figure-skating championships shows exactly how much athletes can get away with. Harding; her ex-husband, Jeff Gilooly; her bodyguard Shawn Eckardt; and three other men planned to attack and injure rival skater Nancy Kerrigan. They hoped to force Kerrigan out of the competition so that Harding would be able to win the championship. Kerrigan was in Detroit, practicing for the competition, when she was savagely beaten with a metal baton above her right knee. Kerrigan was forced to withdraw from the championship because of the injury, and Harding went on to win.

After the plot was uncovered by police, Harding was stripped of her title and banned for life from membership in the United States Figure Skating Association. She was, however, still allowed to participate in the skating competition at the 1994 Winter Olympic Games in Lillihammer, Norway.

Although Harding denied having any prior knowledge of the plot against Kerrigan, she plea-bargained the charges against her. In order to avoid going to jail, Harding pleaded guilty to conspiracy and was sentenced to three years' probation by the judge. She was also required to perform fifty-six hundred hours of community service and to pay more than one hundred thousand dollars in fines.[26]

7

Athletes and Drugs

The pressure on athletes to win at all costs has encouraged some of them to look for ways, any ways, to enhance their performance. Many professional and nonprofessional athletes have turned to drugs, both legal and illegal, to achieve this goal. Although drug use seems to be more widespread at the college and professional levels, there have been reports of increasing drug use by high school athletes as well.[1]

Whereas the recreational drug of choice for the high school age group appears to be alcohol, a study conducted

76

by the National Institute on Drug Abuse reported that about two hundred fifty thousand high school students, both male and female, admitted that they had used steroids—synthetic hormone derivatives—at one point in their lives.[2]

One of the main reasons athletes use these drugs is to gain an edge over their opponents. Drugs that enhance performance in this way are known as additives; they include amphetamines and steroids. What magic does an athlete expect from using drugs? According to Michael Askin, author of *Dying to Win*, "Athletes hope for many things from drugs as performance enhancers. They seek an increase in strength and endurance, a delay to the onset of fatigue, and an increase in their ability to concentrate and tolerate pain."[3]

Other athletes have turned to different drugs to deal with the pain and joint inflammation that are direct results of excessive exercise, body contact, and game-related injuries. These drugs are known as restorative drugs and include aspirin, tranquilizers, and muscle relaxers.[4]

Stopping the Pain

Pain is an accepted part of playing many games. In football, with three-hundred-pound linemen regularly crashing into relatively lightweight quarterbacks, it's easy to see why this is true. Former Buffalo Bill star quarterback Jim Kelly said,

> The game is played with pain. If you can't play in pain, you should be playing golf. . . . There's a lot

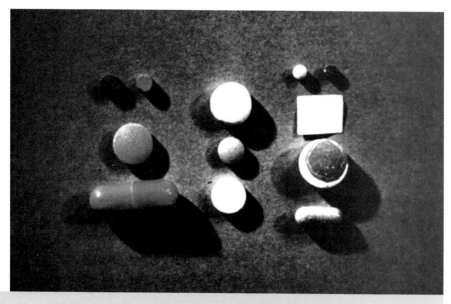

Some athletes use many types of pills to deal with the physical pain that comes with playing professional sports.

at stake. Big contracts, the pressure of losing your job—a lot of things force some guys to do things that maybe they shouldn't do. I know I played in a lot of games that I should not have been playing in but I did.[5]

The abuse of painkillers in the National Football League has become a widespread problem. In fact, the league is taking steps to deal with this abuse. The NFL's monitoring program now includes random, unannounced drug tests of players throughout the entire year, not just during the playing season. To increase drug awareness, the league has also issued guidelines on the use of the prescription drugs that are regularly kept in the teams' locker rooms.

Many rumors are circulated about players who have traded game tickets with pharmaceutical company representatives for drugs. The misuse of painkillers by team trainers and doctors is also widely suspected. The main reason for this abuse is the constant pressure on players to be able to continue to play throughout an entire season.

The use of painkilling drugs can be addictive. Quarterback Brett Favre of the 1997 Super Bowl champion Green Bay Packers admitted to being addicted to the painkiller Vicodin[TM] and needed to seek medical help for his addiction.[6] An athlete's addiction is often discovered and diagnosed after a playing season has ended, when the athlete, who has regularly been taking drugs, is suddenly cut off from his supply. Such a user will begin to suffer withdrawal symptoms similar to those experienced by people who are trying to stop drinking, smoking, or using other illegal drugs.

A special report that appeared in *The New York Times* on April 13, 1997, shed some light on the widespread secret use of drugs by many players in the NFL: A member of the New York Giants football team told a story about the team's successful 1993 season when the Giants' record was 11–5:

> One veteran guy had a bag full of pills, I mean hundreds and hundreds of pills from painkillers to speed. He didn't get the stuff from the Giants. I think he got them from other doctors. A small group of veterans, maybe six or seven, would take pills before every game.

Then came the playoff game between the Giants and the San Francisco 49ers.

> Before the game . . . guys, like they had done before each game, came for the pills. But he [the supplier] was out of them. There was almost a riot. . . . Then somebody took the bag and started licking the residue at the bottom of the bag.[7]

Despite the efforts of the NFL, prescription drug abuse remains a constant problem with no immediate solution. Even though the misuse of drugs is against NFL policy, as well as illegal, some athletes are still willing to risk legal action, as well as severe medical complications, in order to keep playing.

Amphetamines

In 1970, former star baseball pitcher Jim Bouton wrote *Ball Four*, a book about his career in the major leagues. In the book, Bouton revealed that, in his opinion, as many as 40 percent of the players in major-league baseball took either amphetamines or a combination of amphetamines and barbiturates. During the 1960s and 1970s, amphetamines, in particular, were very popular. Their use was designed to help athletes ignore the pain from their injuries and "get up" for a game.

Anabolic Steroid Use

According to a report prepared by the National Institute on Drug Abuse, athletes in a number of sports, particularly football, have resorted to using anabolic (tissue-building) steroids. These are synthetic hormones that increase both an athlete's muscle bulk and his level of performance. These synthetic chemicals, sometimes popularly referred to as "roids," or "juice," were originally developed in the 1930s to help older men maintain their strength. Steroids help stimulate the growth of both muscle and bone.

Steroids are produced naturally and are present in everyone's body. They help determine sex characteristics, and they aid in the growth of muscle, bone, and skin. However, artificial anabolic steroids are different from natural hormones, and they can be dangerous. Numerous negative side effects can occur from their misuse. These side effects include such minor symptoms as acne, balding, and bad breath. The drugs can also result in more serious side effects such as jaundice, high blood pressure, liver damage, and cancer. Other medical risks, like contracting HIV, can occur from sharing unsterilized needles with fellow users. Still other medical complications, such as heart attacks or strokes, may not appear until later in life, long after the steroid use has ceased.

According to a 1996 United States government study, the illegal manufacturing and selling of steroids has become a $400 million-a-year business. Many of these illegal drugs are manufactured in unclean secret laboratories in the United States and overseas, and the products are sometimes impure or even bogus.[8]

Steroid use can cause emotional as well as physical problems. Doctors are still discovering the effects that steroid use has on behavior. Cases of depression and violent mood swings have been widely reported. While steroid use may cause aggressive behavior, a quality some athletes are seeking, the degree of this aggression cannot always be precisely controlled.

Dave Meggyesy, a former linebacker for the St. Louis (now Arizona) Cardinals made the following comment: "NFL trainers do more dealing than the average junkie." He went on to say that "the violent, brutal NFL player is a 'synthetic product,' a man turned into an animal by large doses of drugs."[9]

Controlling Steroid Use in Sports

The use of steroids by professional athletes in the United States has gained in popularity during the last thirty years. Several decades ago, athletes experimented with both pills and injectable steroids. Dianabol™ was one of the early drugs used by professional athletes. As the pressure for athletes to perform better increased, so did the use of steroids. At one time, it was estimated that half the members of the Dallas Cowboys were using steroids.[10]

Both the federal government and the National Football League decided to take action to reduce steroid use. In 1988, Congress enacted the Anti-Drug Abuse Act. This law made the possession or distribution of steroids for nonmedical purposes a federal offense. Two years later the government passed the Anabolic Steroids Control Act. This law increased the penalties for using steroids and for selling them. Anyone dealing in or actually using steroids could be arrested. Punishment for the possession of steroids would be up to one year in prison. Distribution of steroids would lead to a prison term of up to five years and a fine of $250,000.

The NFL has placed steroids on its list of banned substances. The league currently conducts random drug tests for steroid use. Dennis Byrd, a former defensive player for the New York Jets, revealed that he was tested for steroids nine times during one year, although none of the tests ever gave a positive result. A player who tests positive for steroid use is suspended, but that penalty has still not stopped athletes from using the drugs.

In October 1995, Joel Steed, a defensive lineman for the Pittsburgh Steelers, was handed a four-game suspension by the NFL for testing positive for steroids. Under the league policy for first-time violators, Steed would have to undergo medical exams periodically and could not return to play if he tested positive.[11]

In 1986, the NCAA began a program of testing athletes for eighty-one substances at its championship events. The association acknowledged that about three thousand of these tests would be performed that year at a total cost of $950,000.[12]

According to professor Murray Sperber of Indiana University, the Ohio State University athletic department spent about one hundred fifty thousand dollars drug-testing its athletes in 1986. The University of Tennessee spent one hundred thousand dollars during the same time period, and the president of the University of Wyoming estimated that drug testing there could cost as much as eight hundred dollars per athlete.[13]

Recreational Drug Use

Len Bias, six feet eight inches tall and well built, was an All-Star basketball player at the University of Maryland. He was the second pick in the NBA college player draft of 1986. On June 17, 1986, Bias was chosen by the Boston Celtics, the team with which he had always dreamed of playing. Several days after the draft, Bias mysteriously died of cardiorespiratory arrest—his heart and breathing had stopped—a highly unusual occurrence for a twenty-two-year-old athlete who appeared to be in such excellent physical condition. The autopsy report that was submitted following his death indicated that Bias had died from the use of cocaine.[14]

Illegal cocaine use generally goes unnoticed until a star athlete is arrested or, as in the case of Len Bias, becomes a fatality. According to Bill Conlin, sportswriter for *The Sporting News*,

> Drugs are an invisible problem. You don't see guys passed out in hotel lobbies after snorting cocaine, smoking dope, or popping pills. The nature of the beast is different, far more subtle and with lethal physical and psychological consequences. Drug experiences are not openly discussed on the team bus the way drinking exploits are.[15]

Among both professional and college athletes the

illegal use of what are commonly known as recreational drugs (marijuana, cocaine, and heroin) has increased. According to Rick Telander, author of *The Hundred Yard Lie*, in the sport of football alone, three out of four rushing leaders who played in the Atlantic Coast Conference during the late 1980s were arrested for crimes that included possession of cocaine and conspiracy to distribute cocaine.[16]

More recently, several Dallas Cowboys were suspended for drug violations. In 1996, Leon Lett, a well-known defensive tackle, served a one-year league suspension for violating the NFL's substance-abuse policy. Defensive end Shante Carver missed six

The use of cocaine has become an increasing problem in professional sports. Len Bias, a talented college basketball player, died of a cocaine overdose before he even got a chance to compete in the National Basketball Association.

games of the 1996 season for drug-abuse violations. Clayton Holmes, a cornerback, had a four-game suspension increased to an entire year in 1995, for drug violations. During the 1996 season, All-Star receiver Michael Irvin pleaded no-contest to drug possession charges and received a five-game suspension and four years of court probation.[17] There are thirty teams in the NFL alone, and each team can offer a correspondingly similar roster of drug-abuse problems.

While professional baseball, football, and hockey have addressed the issue of athletes' using drugs and have instituted strict guidelines for drug abusers, basketball has yet to deal with this issue. The NBA is the only one of the four major sports leagues that does not specifically prohibit the use of marijuana as part of a player's basic contract agreement.[18] In addition, in the NBA, only players who have previously been in a drug rehabilitation program are randomly tested for drugs.

A Story of Two Athletes

The pressure to be the best ultimately cost pro football player Lyle Alzado his life. Alzado, who played defensive positions for the Denver Broncos, Cleveland Browns, and Los Angeles Raiders, admitted that he had started taking steroids while in college, first at Kilgore Junior College in Texas and later at Yankton College in South Dakota. He used the drugs to build his muscles so that he would be noticed by pro scouts and hopefully be offered a contract to play in the NFL.

The first steroid Alzado experimented with, Dianabol™, seemed to work. He was able to increase his weight from 190 to 300 pounds by combining a change in diet with taking the steroids. In 1971, Alzado got his first job in the NFL when he replaced an injured teammate on the Denver Broncos. He noticed that the steroids not only improved his size and agility, but made him more aggressive and apparently better able to play. Alzado stated: "I was so wild about winning. It's all I cared about, winning, winning. I never talked about anything else."[19]

Eventually, using the steroids caught up with Alzado. He had been injecting himself with the drugs as well as taking pills orally for ten years. Rarely did he stop taking the drugs to give his body a rest. Most athletes use steroids for six to eight weeks, then stop taking them for an equal amount of time. Allowing for a rest period is known as cycling. Alzado allowed only two weeks between cycles.

Despite doctors' warnings about the possible harmful side effects of taking steroids for a prolonged period, Alzado continued to use the drugs while he played professional football. In 1990, Alzado developed symptoms of dizziness, double vision, and seizures. He was hospitalized and diagnosed with brain cancer. Alzado was treated with chemotherapy. In an interview with Shelley Smith of *Sports Illustrated* magazine, Alzado said:

> This is the hardest thing I've ever done, to admit that I've done something wrong. If I had known

The late Lyle Alzado, who played for the Denver Broncos, Cleveland Browns, and Los Angeles Raiders, built himself up with steroids and later suffered the consequences.

that I would be this sick now, I would have tried to make it in football on my own, naturally. Whoever is doing this stuff, if you stay on it too long . . . you're going to get something bad. . . .[20]

Lyle Alzado died on May 14, 1992. Dr. Robert Huizenga was one of the doctors who treated him. Although it has not been clinically proven, Huizenga believed that Alzado's cancer may have been caused by the use of the steroids.

Steroid abuse has filtered down to the players in America's colleges—with some equally distressing results. Tom Chaikin was a star football player for the University of South Carolina. In order to be a better defensive tackle, he started taking steroids. The use of this drug enabled him to bulk up from 220 to 270 pounds, and he was able to lift five hundred pounds in the weight room. However, the drug's side effects were almost fatal. During his junior year, Tom Chaikin suffered an attack of angina, a heart condition that causes chest pains and numbness in the arms. Chaikin was promptly taken to a local hospital, where it was discovered that he was also suffering from very high blood pressure.[21]

In the fall of 1987, Chaikin locked himself in his dorm room and placed a cocked and loaded .357 magnum revolver under his chin. He was tired of all the side effects, both physical and emotional, resulting from the use of the steroids. Luckily, he was stopped from pulling the trigger by his father, and after spending time in the psychiatric ward of a Maryland hospital, Chaikin went back to college.[22] He got his college degree from the University of

South Carolina in 1988.[23] Tom Chaikin was much luckier than Lyle Alzado.

Ironically, during that same year, Chaikin's defensive line coach, Jim Washburn, was indicted by a grand jury in South Carolina on several drug charges and pleaded guilty to the charge of importing steroids into the state.[24]

During the early 1990s, Dr. Bob Goldman, founder and director of The National Academy of Sports Medicine, conducted a survey of almost two hundred world-class athletes. He asked them whether, if they knew that in five years they would die from the drug's side effects, they would take a powerful drug that would guarantee making them champions. Astonishingly, more than 50 percent of the athletes surveyed said they would still take the dangerous drug.[25]

Steroids in the Olympics

Performance-enhancing drugs have also been linked to Olympic athletes. At first, in Olympic training, the drugs were used mostly by weightlifters. However, as other athletes saw what steroids could do to improve performance, track and field athletes, especially those who participate in the shot put, javelin, and discus events, also started using the drugs. By 1990, it was reported that steroids were being used by competitors in other sports events, including hockey, soccer, swimming, wrestling, and skiing.[26]

As early as 1968, Olympic athletes were being tested for illegal drugs. In 1976, testing for steroids began. Because of the rising use of performance-enhancing drugs, the International Olympic Committee (IOC), the organization that regulates the Olympic Games, formed a medical division to help curb the use of all illegal drugs at Olympic events. The IOC developed a list of drugs to be banned during competition. More recently, the IOC began unannounced random drug testing of Olympic athletes to monitor the enforcement of their rules. During the 1988 summer games in Seoul, South Korea, track star Ben Johnson of Canada was stripped of his gold medal in the 100-meter race and was barred from competition for two years because he tested positive for illegal steroid use during his drug screening. In 1992, during a track meet in Canada, Johnson again tested positive for illegal drug use. He has been banned from competition for life by the International Amateur Athletic Federation.[27]

To reduce drug use by Olympic athletes, the medical chief of the IOC ordered a device known as a spectrometer, which cost six hundred thousand dollars, to be used during the 1996 summer games in Atlanta to detect substance-abusing athletes. The spectrometer works by identifying the patterns of light given off by chemical substances. Using the device, lab technicians can identify the presence of illegal drugs in an athlete's urine.

Blood-Doping

Another technique used by athletes to help improve their performance is known as blood-doping. In this procedure, an athlete has one pint of his own blood taken from him and preserved. The packed red blood cells are then frozen and stored under sterile conditions. At about twenty-four to forty-eight hours before an athletic competition, the blood is returned intravenously to the donor's body. This procedure expands the athlete's normal volume of blood, which increases his stamina. Sometimes a blood substitute is used. The practice of blood-doping has been banned by the International Olympic Committee and other amateur athletic organizations.[28]

Fighting Back

Benji Ramieriz, a high school football player from Ohio, died tragically of a heart attack in 1989. The county coroner who examined Ramieriz's body pronounced that his death was caused, in part, by anabolic steroids.[29]

One of the organizations that is trying to fight back against illegal drug use by athletes is the Parents Association for Youth Sports. PAYS, as the association is familiarly known, publishes a guidebook entitled *A Parent's Guide to Better Sports for Kids . . . Better Kids for Life*. Among the organization's nationwide requirements for youth sports is that parents refrain from using drugs, alcohol, and tobacco at youth sporting events. PAYS believes adults should set a good example for children and make sports participation a positive experience. All children, not just athletes, need to learn at an early age the consequences, both legal and physical, of drug use.

All young people need to learn the importance of saying no to drugs and alcohol, and athletes especially need to be aware of what drugs can do to their bodies. According to Josie Todd, women's varsity basketball coach at the University of Illinois at Urbana-Champaign,

> For the athlete who wants to be the best he or she can be, the answer to the question "why say no" is that drugs [ultimately] hurt athletic performance. And because drugs hinder and prevent optimal performance, they have no value to the dedicated athlete.[30]

8

Positive Role Models and Solutions

The press often tends to focus on the negative actions of professional athletes. In doing so, it passes over some of the good and positive accomplishments of many players. Some professional athletes are indeed the role models that young people and their parents are searching for. One such individual is David Robinson.

Robinson plays basketball for the NBA's San Antonio Spurs. He is a graduate of the United States Naval Academy at Annapolis, Maryland, where he majored in mathematics. In his sophomore year, Robinson was an All-American basketball player. Robinson served his country as an officer in the United States Navy before starting his professional basketball career. In 1996, Robinson was chosen as the NBA's Most Valuable Player.

Robinson is also a born-again Christian whose religious faith has guided his life. Unfortunately, there are some critics who believe that because of Robinson's religion and integrity, he is not mean or aggressive enough to lead his team to a championship season.[1]

Recently Robinson donated $5 million to start a program in San Antonio, Texas, to help educate young people and teach them to become leaders. Professional sports need more players like David Robinson to help restore the ideals of good sportsmanship and personal dignity.

Another positive role model is Dale Murphy. Murphy played professional baseball for both the Atlanta Braves and the Philadelphia Phillies. During his twelve years in Atlanta, he gained a reputation for being the most popular athlete in the state of Georgia. His autographed photo was the one most often requested by fans from his team's public relations office. Murphy doesn't smoke, drink, or curse and is still married to the same woman. He teaches Sunday school, visits hospitals on a regular basis, and rarely refuses to sign autographs. He has also donated time and money to many charities, particularly the Huntington's Disease Society of America.[2]

Many other athletes have given something back to their communities and helped the less fortunate. Tennis star Andre Agassi has donated millions of

David Robinson, a graduate of the United States Naval Academy, is respected for his off-court behavior as well as for his on-court skill.

dollars to children's charities in Las Vegas, Nevada. Reggie White of the Green Bay Packers put up money for a program to help minorities start their own businesses. Mark McGwire, star slugger of the St. Louis Cardinals baseball team, donated $1 million to a program for abused children. Before she died, Olympic gold medalist Florence Griffith Joyner established a special organization to help troubled kids in California.

Finally, the people of the town of Manoguaybo, in the Dominican Republic, have a new church. The Immaculate Conception church, opened in February 1998, is the gift of Pedro Martinez. Martinez is a pitcher for the Boston Red Sox, who donated a portion of his $75 million salary to his hometown for the church's construction.[3]

Solutions

In 1992, the National Football League established the Family Assistance Program to help professional athletes who are undergoing personal problems. The program employs a team that includes professional psychologists, psychiatrists, social workers, and marriage counselors. Domestic violence is one of the main topics that is discussed every year.

A toll-free hot-line phone number is provided to encourage calling for help, and letters are sent to all NFL players before summer training camp reminding them of the availability of this service. During training camp, a coordinator meets with each team and discusses a variety of topics. Domestic violence is one topic that must always be covered. According to Dr. Lem Burnham, NFL vice-president for player and employee development, "Abuse must be addressed because it is easier to prevent a personal problem than solve one. The program tries to not let them [the players] get to that point."[4]

To help prevent sexual assaults by athletes on college campuses, the National Collegiate Athletic Association has also developed a life skills personal development program.

National Sportsmanship Day

In an effort to send a more positive message to young people about sports participation and good sportsmanship, the Institute for International Sport and the Cigna Healthcare Corporation have cosponsored a National Sportsmanship Day for the last eight years. According to David Brennan, director of this event, the purpose of the program is to "promote students' appreciation of the critical roles of ethics, honesty, peaceful conflict resolution, and fair play in athletics and society through education and sport."[5]

In previous years, more than ten thousand schools throughout the United States, as well as schools in more than one hundred countries, have participated in the celebration. Local events include essay and poster contests, guest speakers and discussions, and special athletic activities in schools.

Darrell J. Burnett, an Institute for International Sports Ethics Fellow, has developed a checklist for young people to follow, which will help them develop habits of good sportsmanship. This list includes these guidelines:

1. Abide by the rules of the game.

2. Try to avoid arguments.

3. Always play fair.

4. Respect the efforts of the other team.

5. Accept the judgment calls of the game officials.[6]

Programs like the National Sportsmanship Day send a message to young athletes that by playing fairly by the rules, they can improve their life skills as well as their athletic powers.

9

Rule Changes and Solutions

The increase in the number of incidents of sports violence in the United States, as well as in foreign countries, has been significant during the past twenty-five years. Young athletes are taught from an early age to be aggressive. Their parents and coaches drill into their heads the importance, sometimes even the necessity, of winning and being number one. The principles and traditions of good sportsmanship and pure athleticism, which once guided the terms of play, are quickly being lost. Nowadays the modern temptations to achieve a macho image and

100

a high salary are paramount. Hundreds of current and former athletes have been crippled, both physically and emotionally, as a result of aggressive play in their sports.

Away from the ballfields, hockey rinks, and basketball courts, some athletes have battered their wives and girlfriends, bought and sold drugs, and created risks to their communities. Although several of these athletes have ended up in prison, the majority have been treated as special cases, beyond the reach of our legal system.

In addition, the loyal followers of athletes—their fans—have trashed stadiums and destroyed neighborhoods, killed innocent bystanders, and caused tens of millions of dollars' worth of damage to both public and private property.

In a nation where sports are such a vital part of the culture, how do we begin to institute changes that will make athletics safer and more enjoyable for players and spectators alike? Assuming there are still ways to create a fairer and more sportsmanlike environment, another question remains: Do today's fans really want more sportsmanlike conditions, or are they really after the thrill of violence and physical danger in their games?

According to Robert Yeager, author of *Seasons of Shame*, "If we hope to reduce violence in our sports, changes must be initiated in . . . distinct areas; game rules and penalties, playing gear and equipment . . . and above all, our own attitudes and expectations."[1]

What's Been Done

One possibility frequently discussed by officials, coaches, and players is changing the rules and penalties of games to help protect athletes from more serious injuries. The current system of meting out fines and suspensions does not seem to deter, to any significant extent, the number of violent incidents that take place. Sports psychologist Thomas Tutko recommends a total revamping of game penalties with a specific emphasis on reducing injuries.

Some strict rules have recently been put in place in several sports with this goal in mind. For example, in baseball, if a runner deliberately slides into an opponent, or a pitcher throws a ball too close to the batter, or two or more players fight, the offending party can be subjected to a fine or an ejection from the game.

During the 1977 basketball season, Rudy Tomjanovich of the Houston Rockets had his face brutally injured by Kermit Washington during a game. But it wasn't until 1993 that the NBA passed a rule change that punished a player with a suspension if he fought with an opposing player. The commissioner of the NBA has also levied heavy fines against players who fight during games. However, since most of the players in the NBA make millions of dollars a year, the fines are no real deterrent. Back in 1978, a third referee was added to help reduce the number of violent acts occurring on the courts.[2] However, this measure also seems to have failed to reduce fighting during games.

Officials from the NHL have also taken some steps to reduce the outbreaks of fighting on the rinks. An example is the "third man in" rule. If a (third or more) player comes off the bench to join in a fight already in progress on the ice, he is given a game "misconduct." Upon review of his actions, the player can be suspended for up to several games. Certain penalties have also been increased if an offender draws blood as a result of his infraction. As is the case in basketball, there is little evidence to prove that such toothless rule changes have materially altered fighting in hockey games.

Team Goals

Each year the team owners of the NFL meet to discuss possible rule changes. Their collective goal is to try to make the game more exciting and to keep the fans coming to the stadiums.

Several years ago the league decided to change the kickoff point, from the thirty-five-yard line to the thirty-yard line. By making this change, the team receiving the ball would almost always have to return the kickoff rather than let the ball sail into the end zone. According to former NFL player Jack Tatum,

> Thus you have the excitement of twenty-two bodies building up full heads of speed and slamming into each other. . . . Returning kick-offs [sic] is dangerous, and covering kick-offs is dangerous, but because it is exciting, some whiz who sits behind a desk in an office decides to move the kicking team back five yards to ensure the kick return.[3]

Although hockey players are often sent to the penalty box, existing penalties do not seem stiff enough to seriously curtail fighting on the ice.

Other changes that had been made in an effort to protect NFL players included requiring the referees to whistle the end of play earlier in order to cut down on late and illegal hits, and to prohibit head-butting and spearing (ramming one's helmet into the stomach or back of an opposing player).[4]

In 1994, the NFL asked its competition committee to look into the possibility of instituting penalty boxes, much like those used in the National Hockey League, during football games. According to the NFL's director of communications, such a proposal would be aimed at resisting "flagrant hits on the quarterback, but not for other penalties. It would have to be determined how long a player would have to spend in the penalty box, whether it's for a specific amount of time or a certain number of plays." There were many opposed to this suggestion, claiming there were already rules in place to deal with the issue of protecting quarterbacks. For example, an NFL referee can, at his own discretion, eject any player from a game for overly aggressive actions. "The trick for the competition committee would be to curb the unnecessary violence without changing the way the game is played."[5]

In his book, *Seasons of Shame*, Robert Yaeger suggests that in the past, violence has paid off for the players. He believes that the violent bullies of the game need to be expelled. He said, "The entire sports world is disgraced when a football player can openly slug two opponents in succession and return to competition without so much as an unsportsmanlike-conduct penalty."[6]

Equipment Changes

In the sport of professional boxing, the debate continues about whether boxers should be required to wear protective headgear. After twenty-eight-year-old John Montantes died as a result of head injuries, the Nevada State Athletic Commission considered whether to institute a new rule. Dr. Elias Ghanem, the commissioner, felt that wearing headgear would detract from the sport of boxing and that people would stop coming to matches. Another athletic commission member agreed: "Pro fighters don't want to wear it [the helmet], and from a marketing standpoint, fans want to see the fighters' faces."[7]

Suggestions for Youth Sports

Dr. John Baker, an orthopedic surgeon who also serves as team physician for a high school football team in New Jersey, insists changes in equipment are the key to maintaining player safety. The most frequent injuries to high school football players are sprained ankles, contusions to the pelvic area, sprained knees and ligaments, and concussions. Hip pointers, painful bruises to the hip and pelvic area, are also a common problem. Adding an additional layer of padding to football helmets, for example, could help reduce concussions. On the other hand, rule changes that prohibit using the helmet as a weapon (by using it to ram an opposing player in the chest or back) have also served to reduce chest and spinal cord injuries, like those to Daryl Stingley and Marc Buoniconti.[8]

The use of a knee brace, once popular in football circles, is currently discouraged because it can lock a player's knee in a fixed position. It can cause serious injury if a player is hit from the blind side or doesn't have enough time to plant his foot correctly.

Baker also felt that poor coaching and inadequate physical preparedness are contributing to high school football injuries. However, he stressed that the positive aspects of playing a sport far outweigh the negatives. Baker said, "Athletics teach about life. That's why I'm involved in it. Playing sports in

Strong, well fitting equipment can prevent some injuries to young football players.

school teaches about hard work, effort, and winning and losing."[9]

Preventing Sports Injuries

According to the National Safe Kids Campaign, more than 3 million children between the ages of five and fourteen suffer from sports- and recreation-related injuries each year in the United States. More than seven hundred fifty thousand of them end up being treated in hospital emergency rooms. Injuries to young people account for 40 percent of all sports-related injuries.

1996 Sports Injuries to Children Aged 5–14	
Sport	**Injuries**
Basketball	200,000
Football	165,000
Baseball/Softball	105,000

Source: National Safe Kids Campaign fact sheet

In youth programs, baseball is considered the most dangerous sport because it has the highest fatality rate. This is due in part to the fact that brain injury is the major cause of sports-related deaths, and a significant number of baseball injuries are caused by being hit in the head with a ball.

What can young athletes do to reduce the threat

of a sports-related injury? Here is a list of tips to help them stay safe:

1. Be sure that you are in good physical condition. See your family doctor for a checkup before you start to play.

2. Wear the proper safety equipment at all times.

3. Play in a program supervised by adults with athletes of your own age and ability.

4. Eat healthful foods.

5. Warm up before playing in a game.

6. Avoid illegal drugs and alcohol.

Despite all the precautions, sometimes a tragedy cannot be prevented. Travis Roy loved to play ice hockey ever since he was a boy in Maine. On October 20, 1995, eleven seconds into his first game as a Boston University hockey player, Roy lost his balance after checking Mitch Vig of the University of North Dakota into the boards (forcefully pushing him into the side of rink). Roy's head hit the boards, causing a cracked fourth vertebra. The injury has left him paralyzed. He will probably never walk again.[10]

10

What Do You Think?

Participation in sports has become a beloved and intrinsic part of our culture. Sports can be a great asset for young people. They help develop physical fitness and build character. They help teach life's lessons about teamwork, cooperation, and following directions. They also teach us how to deal with defeat. Nevertheless, sports can be deadly for those who play, as well as for some who watch.

So far, there has been no public outcry to reduce violence on the field at sporting events. Neither has there been any governmental effort to eliminate street celebrations when a local team wins a championship, although these celebrations are notorious for causing property damage, and death and injuries to innocent bystanders. It seems that most people like their sports the way they are.

Some people will tell you that violence in sports is simply part of the game. After all, our very nation was founded by undergoing a violent, bloody revolution. Today our society reflects that tumultuous beginning: We are confronted daily with an epidemic of shootings and other violent acts in our cities, towns, and schools. Even our Capitol building in Washington, D.C., is no longer safe from gunmen. Is it possible that the great success of America's current sports scene may simply be a by-product of our society's vicious streak?

Other people will add that the serious and debilitating injuries that players receive are a necessary and integral part of our games, acknowledged and even expected by the players when they sign with a team. Clearly, one reason players demand and receive such large salaries is to compensate them in advance for any injuries and disabilities they may have to endure later on.

Some people, however, are calling for a change. This group includes many sports psychologists and orthopedic surgeons who witness daily the price athletes pay, both physically and emotionally, for their participation in violent and aggressive sports. These people who look forward to changing the rules and penalties want sports to be safer. They wish to change our perception of sports stars, superheroes, and idols. In addition, they want to redirect the focus of team athletics to the principles of fairness and good sportsmanship.

Are these goals still attainable in our modern cauldron of hype, greed, and idolotry? Are our nation's athletes trapped, like so many gladiators, in our widespread syndrome of violence? Or is there still hope for good sportsmanship and fair play?

What do you think?

Glossary

amphetamines—Drugs that increase physical and mental activity. They are sometimes called "pep pills" or "bennies." They are illegal unless prescribed by a doctor.

anabolic steroids—A group of man-made substances that imitate hormones found naturally in the body. They are used by some athletes to build muscle mass and provide extra stamina.

barbiturates—A class of drugs used to calm people or help them sleep.

blood doping—Removing a person's own blood and saving it for future transfusions. This procedure helps build up the oxygen level in the blood.

concussion—An injury to the brain caused by a trauma to the head.

Dianabol™—A steroid used by some professional athletes, particularly football players, to help improve their performance.

domestic violence—Violent acts committed by men or women against their spouses, relatives, or friends.

dopamine—A chemical occurring naturally in the human brain. It is needed for normal brain activity.

performance-enhancing drugs—Drugs taken by athletes to help them excel on the field by increasing their strength or stamina.

postconcussion syndrome—A group of symptoms caused by receiving a second concussion before a prior one has had a chance to heal.

spectrometer—An instrument used to determine whether illegal drugs have been taken. It uses light to measure the presence of chemicals in the urine.

syndrome—A group of signs and symptoms that occur together and usually form an identifiable pattern.

Vicodan™—A drug that reduces pain. It is taken by some athletes so that they can continue to play even if they are injured.

Resources

For information on gear to prevent athletic injuries
The National SAFE KIDS Campaign
1301 Pennsylvania Avenue, NW
Suite 1000, Washington, DC 20004-1707

For help with a drug problem
The National Institute on Drug Abuse
Confidential hotline
1-800-662-HELP

The National Clearinghouse for Alcohol
and Drug Information
P.O. Box 2345
Rockville, MD 30852
1-800-729-6686

**For information on National Sportsmanship Day
and ways to promote fair play and sportsmanship**
Institute for International Sport
University of Rhode Island
306 Adams Hall
P.O. Box 104
Kingston, RI 02881
(401) 874-2550

National Alliance for Youth Sports
2050 Vista Parkway
West Palm Beach, FL 33411
1-800-688-KIDS
(561) 684-1141

Chapter Notes

Chapter 1. Introduction

1. D. Stanley Eitzen and George H. Sage, *Sociology of American Sport* (Dubuque, Iowa: William C. Brown Communications., 1982), p. 67.

2. Dan Atyeo, *Blood and Guts: Violence in Sports* (New York: Paddington Press, Ltd., 1979), p. 328.

3. Wilbert Leonard, *A Sociological Perspective of Sport*, 2nd ed. (Minneapolis, Minn.: Burgess Publishing Company, 1984), p. 333.

4. Melvin H. Williams, *Drugs and Athletic Performance* (Springfield, Ill.: Charles C. Thomas Publisher, Ltd., 1974), p. vii.

5. Arnold R. Beisser, *The Madness in Sports* (New York: Appleton-Century-Crofts, 1967), pp. 156–57.

Chapter 2. A Short History of Violence in Sports

1. Michael Poliakoff, *Combat Sports in the Ancient World* (New Haven: Yale University Press, 1987) p. 54.

2. Chester G. Star, *The World Book Encyclopedia*, vol. 8, 1986, p. 196.

3. Walter Umminger, *Supermen, Heroes, and Gods* (London: Thames and Hudson, 1963), p. 73.

4. J. J. Sanders, *The World Book Encyclopedia*, vol. 11, 1986, pp. 276–77.

5. Stephen Figler, *Sports and Play in American Life* (Philadelphia: Saunders College Publishing, 1981), p. 199.

Chapter 3. Violence in Pro Sports

1. The Mike Utley Foundation, "Thumbs Up! Mike Utley Biography," 1997, <http://www.imageone.com/Mikeutley/utley2.html> (December 23, 1992).

2. Steve Wilstein, "NFL's Probe Has an Impact," *The Los Angeles Times*, November 30, 1997, sports section, p. 1.

3. Peter King, "The Unfortunate 500," *Sports Illustrated*, December 7, 1992, pp. 20–25.

4. Peter Alfano, "Battling Athletes Hurt Sports' Image," *The New York Times*, February 8, 1988, pp. C1-4.

5. Jack McCallum and Dan Yeager, "I Know He's Gone Off Before," *Sports Illustrated*, April 29, 1996, pp. 38–41.

6. "Kick to Cost Rodman in a Huge Way," *The Philadelphia Inquirer*, January 18, 1997, p. C1.

7. Dan Atyeo, *Blood and Guts: Violence in Sports* (New York: Paddington Press, Ltd., 1979), p. 237.

8. Wilbert Leonard, *A Sociological Perspective of Sport*, 2nd ed. (Minneapolis, Minn.: Burgess Publishing Company, 1984), p. 333.

9. Jack McCallum, "Way Out of Control," *Sports Illustrated*, May 23, 1994, p. 28.

10. Tim Graham, "Boxer Loses Battle For Life," *Las Vegas Sun*, September 29, 1997 <http://www.lasvegassun.com/s...ories/archives/1997/sep/29/56340340.html> (October 15, 1998).

11. Jon Saraceno, "Tyson Faces Disciplinary Hearing . . ." *USA Today*, June 30, 1997, p. C1.

12. Rick Telander, "Point After: Muhammad Ali is Brain-Damaged," *Sports Illustrated*, July 1, 1991, pp. 75–78.

13. *Journal of the American Medical Association*, vol. 273, January 14, 1983, p. 256.

14. Hank Hersch, "It's War Out There," *Sports Illustrated*, July 20, 1987, pp. 14–17.

Chapter 4. Sports Violence and Young People

1. "Mission and Management of Little League Baseball," Little League Online, 1988, <http://www.littleleague.org> (October 15, 1998).

2. "Academics and Athletics Go Hand in Hand," Pop Warner Official Rules, n.d., <http://www.dickbutkus.com/dbfn/popwarner> (October 15, 1998).

3. Gilda Berger, *Violence and Sports* (New York: Franklin Watts Inc., 1990), pp. 75–77.

4. Dr. Barry Maron, L.C. Polic, J.A. Kaplan, and F.R. Mueller, "Blunt Impact to the Chest Leading to Sudden Death from Cardiac Arrest During Sports Activities," *New England Journal of Medicine*, June 1995, Vol. 333, pp. 337–342.

5. Susan Fitzgerald, "Heads Up on Soccer Safety," *The Philadelphia Inquirer*, September 16, 1996, p. E1.

6. Peter King, "Halt the Head-Hunting," *Sports Illustrated*, December 19, 1994, p. 46.

7. Ibid.

8. Michael Yaple and Tom Davis, "Pinelands Officials Demand Probe . . ." *The Press of Atlantic City*, September 19, 1996, p. A1, p. A10.

9. Marcia C. Smith, "Ref is Punched: Dobbins Player Arrested," *The Philadelphia Inquirer*, January 8, 1997, p. E8.

10. Bill Lyon, "Youths Learning the Wrong Lesson," *The Philadelphia Inquirer*, January 10, 1997, p. C1.

11. Wilbert Leonard, *A Sociological Perspective of Sport*, 2nd ed. (Minneapolis, Minn.: Burgess Publishing Company, 1984), p. 337.

12. Tony Wharton, "Sacked, Junior Team Banned from Playoffs," *The Virginian-Pilot*, November 19, 1990, p. C5.

13. Elaine Rose, "Beleaguered," *The Press of Atlantic City*, May, 31, 1997, pp. B1–2.

14. Roberty Yeager, *Seasons of Shame* (New York: Mcgraw-Hill Co., 1979), p. 200.

15. Jack Tatum, *They Call me Assassin* (New York: Everest House, 1979), p. 101.

16. Peter Alfano, "Battling Athletes Hurt Sports' Image," *The New York Times*, February 8, 1988, pp. C1-4.

17. William Rhoden, "Big East to Discuss Fighting," *The New York Times*, February 23, 1988, p. A25.

18. Southwest Athletic Conference Home Page, n.d., <http://www.swacpage.com/bands/index/.htm> (October 29, 1988).

Chapter 5. Fan Violence

1. Sally Jenkins, "Savage Assault," *Sports Illustrated*, May, 10, 1993, pp. 18–21.

2. Ibid.

3. Jennifer McGurgan, "Athletic Events, Alcohol, Have Fans Fighting in the Stands," *The Orion*, Vol. 34, Issue 9, March 29, 1995, <http://orion.csuchico.edu/archives/volume34/issue9/sports/aeahffttst.html> (February 5, 1999).

4. Mike Claffey, Anne Kornblut, Jane Furse, "After Bout, Riot at the Ring," *New York Daily News*, July 12, 1996, pp. 4–5.

5. Rick Telander, "Violent Victory," *Sports Illustrated*, November 8, 1993, pp. 60–64.

6. Ibid.

7. Associated Press, Big Ten Conference Feature Page, n.d., <http://www.Nando.net> (September 29, 1996).

8. Marcia Smith, "Brawl in Central Stands Delays. . .," *The Philadelphia Inquirer*, January 30, 1997, p. E7.

9. Sam Carchidi, "Disturbance Mars Atlantic City's Upset . . ." *The Philadelphia Inquirer*, March 8, 1997, p. C7.

10. Doug Glass, "Teen Charged in Fatal Shootings . . .," *San Diego Daily Transcript*, September 27, 1985, <http://www.sddt.com> (October 15, 1998).

11. William O. Johnson, "The Agony of Victory," *Sports Illustrated*, July 5, 1993, pp. 31–37.

12. Ibid.

13. Ibid.

14. Clive Gammon, "A Day of Horror and Shame," *Sports Illustrated*, June 10, 1985, pp. 22–27.

15. Ateyo, p. 160.

16. Peter Alfano, "Battling Athletes Hurt Sports' Image," *The New York Times*, February 8, 1988, pp. C1–4.

17. Wilbert Leonard, *A Sociological Perspective of Sport*, 2nd ed. (Minneapolis, Minn.: Burgess Publishing Company, 1984), p. 324.

18. Nathan Seppa, "Team Spirit Spills Over Into Real Life for Fans," *American Psychological Association Monitor*, July 1996, p. 7.

19. McGurgan.

20. Craig Neff, "Can It Happen in the U.S.," *Sports Illustrated*, June 10, 1985, p. 27.

Chapter 6. Violence Off the Field

1. Harry Stein, "Nike Ad Reminds Parents of Their Responsibilities," *TV Guide*, Vol. 41, issue 25, June 19, 1993, p. 35.

2. Mark Starr, "Cowboys Will Be Boys," *Newsweek*, January 13, 1997, p. 58.

3. Ibid.

4. Ibid.

5. Ron Reid, "Hill Aims to Direct Cowboys on the Road to Best Behavior," *The Philadelphia Inquirer*, April 6, 1997, p. C6.

6. Ray Kennedy, "Pittsburgh Fats Dodges a Silver Bullet," *Sports Illustrated*, March 7, 1977, pp. 24–26, p. 31.

7. "Barkley Charged in Orlando Fight," *USA Today*, December 19, 1997, p. C3.

8. Murray Sperber, *College Sports Inc.* (New York: Henry Holt and Company, 1990), p. 272.

9. Ibid., pp. 272–273.

10. Ibid., p. 272.

11. Karla Haworth, "Athletics Notes," *Chronicle of Higher Education*, March 7, 1997, p. A42.

12. Ibid.

13. Ibid.

14. William Nack and Lester Munson, "Sports' Dirty Secrets," *Sports Illustrated*, July 31, 1995, pp. 62–74.

15. Steve Sneddon, "Commission Takes Stand; Executive Director: 'Integrity' Affirmed," *USA Today*, July 10, 1997, p. C3.

16. Timothy W. Smith, "A Dream Destroyed," *The New York Times*, July 5, 1998, Section 8, p. 1, p. 6.

17. Nack and Munson, pp. 62–74.

18. Ibid.

19. Ibid.

20. Ibid.

21. Ibid.

22. Ibid.

23. Timothy W. Smith, "Notebook," *The New York Times*, December 10, 1995, p. 26.

24. Nack and Munson, pp. 62–74.

25. Sperber, p. 272.

26. Johnette Howard, "Harding in on Plot," *The Washington Post*, March 22, 1994, p. 1, p. 7.

Chapter 7. Athletes and Drugs

1. Melvin H. Williams, *Drugs and Athletic Performance* (Springfield, Ill.: Charles C. Thomas Publisher., Ltd., 1974), p. 7.

2. Karen Judson, *Sports and Money, It's a Sellout!* (Springfield, N.J.: Enslow Publishers, Inc., 1995), p. 27.

3. Michael J. Asken, *Dying to Win* (Washington, D.C.: Acropolis Books, Inc., 1988), p. 53.

4. Wilbert Leonard, *A Sociological Perspective of Sport*, 2nd ed. (Minneapolis, Minn.: Burgess Publishing Company, 1984), p. 128.

5. Mike Freeman, "Painkillers and Addiction Are Prevalent in N.F.L.," *The New York Times*, April 13, 1997, Section 8, p. 1, p. 4.

6. Ibid.

7. Ibid.

8. "Anabolic Steroids, a Threat to Body and Mind," National Institute on Drug Abuse, Community and Professional Branch, Office of Policy and External Affairs, Washington, D.C., 1996, p. 2.

9. Leonard, p. 131.

10. Charles Yesalis, *Anabolic Steroids in Sport and Exercise* (Champaign, Ill.: Human Kinetics Publishers, Inc., 1993), p. 194.

11. "Steed Suspended for Steroid Use," The News and Observer Pub. Co. fr. AP Wire Service, October 23, 1995, <http://www.news-observer.com> (November 30, 1998).

12. Ibid.

13. Murray Sperber, *College Sports Inc.* (New York: Henry Holt and Company, 1990), p. 118.

14. Asken, pp. 40, 53, 69.

15. Bill Conlin, "Detecting Drug Abuse Isn't Easy," *The Sporting News*, October 10, 1981, p. 21.

16. Rick Telander, *The Hundred Yard Lie* (New York, Simon & Schuster, 1989), p. 191.

17. Mark Starr, "Cowboys Will Be Boys," *Newsweek*, January 13, 1997, p. 58.

18. Tim Dwyer, "Commentary," *The Philadelphia Inquirer*, August 6, 1997, p. E1.

19. Lyle Alzado, "I'm Sick and I'm Scared," *Sports Illustrated*, July 2, 1990, pp. 36–40.

20. Ibid.

21. Telander, pp. 60–64.

22. Ibid.

23. Ibid.

24. Ibid.

25. Bob Goldman, *Death in the Locker Room II* (Chicago: Elite Sports Medicine Publications, 1992), pp. 24, 37.

26. Yesalis, p. 40.

27. Judson, p. 32.

28. Williams, p. 171.

29. Goldman, p. 24.

30. Asken, p. 180.

Chapter 8. Positive Role Models and Solutions

1. Chuck Colson, "David Robinson and True Sportsmanship; Virtue Versus Violence," *Breakpoint*, July 1996 <http://www.Breakpoint.org/archives.htm> (November 30, 1998).

2. Mike Capuzzo, "Apple Pie, Motherhood and Dale Murphy," *The Philadelphia Inquirer*, September 4, 1990, p. D1.

3. Gerry Callahan, "Giving Back," *Readers Digest*, August 1998, pp. 155–156.

4. Gene Upshaw and Esta Soler, "The NFL Addresses Domestic Violence," Family Violence Prevention Fund <http://www.igc.org/fund/men/officials.html#nfl> (November 30, 1998).

5. David Brennan, "Packet Overview," *National Sportsmanship Day Information Packet*, Institute for International Sport, Spring 1998, p. 2.

6. Darrell J. Burnett, "Teaching Kids to Be 'Good Sports,'" *National Sportsmanship Day Information Packet*, Institute for International Sport, Spring 1998, pp. 6–7.

Chapter 9. Rule Changes and Solutions

1. Robert Yeager, *Seasons of Shame* (New York: McGraw-Hill Co., 1979), p. 219.

2. Wilbert Leonard, *A Sociological Perspective of Sport*, 2nd ed. (Minneapolis, Minn.: Burgess Publishing Company, 1984), p. 339.

3. Jack Tatum, *They Call Me Assassin* (New York: Everest House Publishers, 1979), p. 229.

4. Yeager, p. 221.

5. Timothy Smith, "N.F.L. May Consider Using a Penalty Box," *The New York Times*, November 29, 1994, p. B17.

6. Yeager, p. 223.

7. Tim Graham, "Boxer Loses Battle for Life," *Las Vegas Sun*, September 29, 1997 <http://lasvegassun.com/ s...ories/archives/1997/sep/29/56340340.html> (October 15, 1998).

8. Dr. John Baker, personal interview, August 14, 1996.

9. Ibid.

10. "College Hockey: Roy Talks About Injury, Life After Accident," Associated Press, March 14, 1996, <http://nando.net/newsroom/ap/oth/1966/oth/mor/feat/ archive/031296/mor1299.html> (January 29, 1998).

Further Reading

Askin, Michael J. *Dying to Win*. Washington, D.C.: Acropolis Books, Ltd., 1988.

Ateyo, Don. *Blood and Guts: Violence in Sports*. New York: Paddington Press, Ltd., 1979.

Beisser, Arnold R. *The Madness in Sports*. New York: Appleton-Century-Crofts, 1967.

Berger, Gilda. *Violence and Sports*. New York: Franklin Watts Inc., 1990.

Bissinger, H. C. *Friday Night Lights: A Town, a Team, and a Dream*. Reading, Mass.: Addison-Wesley Publishing Co., 1990.

Eitzen, Stanley D., and George H. Sage. *Sociology of American Sport*. Dubuque, Iowa: William C. Brown Co., 1982.

Goldman, Bob. *Death in the Locker Room II*. Chicago: Elite Sports Medicine Publications, 1992.

Guttmann, Allen. *Sports Spectators*. New York: Columbia University Press, 1986.

Hauser, Thomas. *Muhammad Ali, His Life and Times*. New York: Touchstone Books, 1991.

Judson, Karen. *Sports and Money: It's a Sellout!* Springfield, N.J.: Enslow Publishers, Inc., 1995.

King, Peter. *Inside the Helmet: A Player's View of the NFL*. New York: Simon & Schuster, 1983.

Kramer, Jerry. *Instant Replay: The Green Bay Diary of Jerry Kramer*. New York: World Publishing Co., 1968.

Lukas, Scott E., Ph.D. *Steroids*. Springfield, N.J.: Enslow Publishers, Inc., 1994.

Meggyesy, Dave. *Out of Their League*. Berkeley, Calif.: Ramparts Press, Inc., 1970.

Messner, Michael. *Power at Play: Sports and the Problem of Masculinity*. Boston: Beacon Press, 1992.

Morris, Eugene. "Mercury," *Against the Grain*. New York: McGraw-Hill & Co., 1988.

Poliakoff, Michael. *Combat Sports in the Ancient World*. New Haven, Conn.: Yale University Press, 1987.

Sperber, Murray. *College Sports Inc*. New York: Henry Holt and Company, 1990.

Tatum, Jack. *They Call Me Assassin*. New York: Everest House Publishers, 1979.

Telander, Rick. *The Hundred Yard Lie: The Corruption of College Football and What We Can Do to Stop It*. New York: Simon & Schuster, 1989.

Williams, Melvin, H. *Drugs and Athletic Performance*. Springfield, Ill.: Charles C. Thomas Publishers, 1974.

Yeager, Robert. *Seasons of Shame*. New York: McGraw Hill & Co., 1979.

Yesalis, Charles E., ed. *Anabolic Steroids in Sports and Exercise*. Champaign, Ill.: Human Kinetics Publishers, 1993.

Internet Addresses

Drug-Free Resource Net: Steroids
<http://www.drugfreeamerica.org/steroids.html>

Institute for International Sport
<http://www.internationalsport.com>

Little League Baseball
<http://www.littleleague.org>

Major League Baseball
<http://www.majorleaguebaseball.com>

National Basketball Association
<http://www.nba.com>

National Football League
<http://www.nfl.com>

National Hockey League
<http://www.nhl.com>

Pop Warner Football
<http://www.dickbutkus.com/dbfn/popwarner>

Sports Illustrated
<http://www.cnnsi.com>

Index

DATE D

NOV 0 1 2001

NOV 0 8 2003

AUG 1 4 2013

OCT 1 1 2021

OCT 1 1 2021

PCL # 106559305 HC2

209467974 ISU

PRINTED IN U.S.A.

GAYLORD